PUT ON YOUR
OWL EYES

Open Your Senses & Discover Nature's Secrets

DEVIN *"Green Frog"* FRANKLIN

Storey Publishing

The mission of Storey Publishing is to serve our customers by publishing practical information that encourages personal independence in harmony with the environment.

With special thanks to my teachers, and everyone in Flying Deer Nature Center's community. Also to Rebecca Sadlon for her editing expertise and her passion for this project, and to Michelle Apland most of all, for her loving support and trusted companionship in creating nature-centered community where all are welcome.

— Devin Franklin

EDITED BY Deborah Burns
ART DIRECTION AND BOOK DESIGN BY Alethea Morrison
TEXT PRODUCTION BY Erin Dawson
INDEXED BY Samantha Miller

Storey books are available for special premium and promotional uses and for customized editions. For further information, please call 800-793-9396.

Storey Publishing
210 MASS MoCA Way
North Adams, MA 01247
storey.com

Printed in China by R.R. Donnelley
10 9 8 7 6 5 4 3 2 1

Library of Congress Cataloging-in-Publication Data on file

COVER PHOTOGRAPHY BY Mars Vilaubi (back, author and bottom center); © Jonathan Knowles/Getty Images (back, top center); © PhotoAlton/Jerome Gorin/Getty Images (back, bottom left); © Cavan Images/Getty Images (back, top left); © GlobalStock/istock.com (front, girl); © borchee/iStock.com (back, top right); © Foryou13/iStock.com (front, rock)

COVER ILLUSTRATIONS BY © Katie Vernon/Lilla Rogers Studio (front); Serafina Velázquez (front, small map); Xavi Velázquez (back, bottom right)

INTERIOR PHOTOGRAPHY BY © Aaron McCoy/Getty Images, 121; © Adriana Varela Photography/Getty Images, 65; © andipantz/iStock.com, 39 middle left; © Andrew Bertuleit/iStock.com, 9; Anthony Intraversato/Unsplash, 54; Anthony Roberts/Unsplash, 92 top; © antic/stock.adobe.com, 22; © Arterra/Getty Images, 100; © Berggren, Hans/Getty Images, 21; © Bobbushphoto/iStock.com, 1; © borchee/iStock.com, 4; © Bryant Aardema -bryants wildlife images/Getty Images, 19; © CampPhoto/iStock.com, 46; © Carlina Teteris/Getty Images, 25 row 3 left; Casey Horner/Unsplash, 32; © Cavan Images/Getty Images, 15; © chas53/iStock.com, 99 (songbird); © Chase Dekker Wild-Life Images/Getty Images, 60 top; © chengyuzheng/iStock.com, 43 bottom; © Chris Carroll/Getty Images, 31; Ciocan Ciprian/Unsplash, 53; © Cyndi Monaghan/Getty Images, 125; © Danita Delimont/Getty Images, 85; © David Crespo/Getty Images, 25 row 2 right; David Morris/Unsplash, 80; Denys Nevozhai/Unsplash, 37; © Design Pics Inc/Alamy Stock Photo, 39 bottom left; © endlessadventure/iStock.com, 72 left; © epantha/iStock.com, 7, 45 top; © fergregory/Adobe Stock, 68; © ferrantraite/Getty Images, 38; © Flashpop/Getty Images, 95; © GlobalP/iStock.com, 99 (squirrel and fox); © grbender/iStock.com, Exploration titles 84, 91, 96; Haley Phelps/Unsplash, 23; © Hannele Lahti, 25 row 3 center; © Hans Neleman/Getty Images, 16; © HansUntch/iStock.com, 69; © Hiyoman/iStock.com, 24; © hocus-focus/Getty Images, note paper backgrounds 28, 29, 51, 71, 90, 103; © imacoconut/iStock.com, 106; © Image Source/Getty Images, 25 row 3 right; © Imgorthand/iStock.com, 88; © James O'Neil/Getty Images, 90; © Jodi Griggs/Getty Images, 114; © Johner Images/Getty Images, 20; © Jonathan Knowles/Getty Images, 86; Josh Power/Unsplash, 115; © JoyTasa/iStock.com, Exploration titles 14, 17, 22; © karlumbriaco/iStock.com, 72 right; Karsten Wurth/Unsplash, 25 row 4 center; Keith Luke/Unsplash, 48; © Kelly Sillaste/Getty Images, 113; © LARISA SHPINEVA/iStock.com, 45 bottom; © lee181077/iStock.com, Exploration titles 111, 116, 122; © Leonid Lazarev/Getty Images, 64; © LOVE_LIFE/iStock.com, 43 top, 44 bottom; Mack Fox Musicfox/Unsplash, 58; © makasana/iStock.com, 101; © Manuela Schewe-Behnisch/EyeEm/Getty Images, 47; © MarioGuti/iStock.com, 39 bottom right; © Marji Lang/Getty Images, 25 row 1; © Mars Vilaubi, 27, 40, 77, 127; Mars Vilaubi, 60 bottom, 61, 92 middle and bottom, 102, 123; Max Saeling/Unsplash, 50; © Melissa Farlow/Getty Images, 25 row 2 left; © mlorenzphotography/Getty Images, 18; © MoreISO/iStock.com, 103; © NNehring/iStock.com, 93; © NoDerog/iStock.com, 39 top; © Olaf Simon/iStock.com, 51; © Owl_photographer/iStock.com, 39 middle right; © PhotoAlton/Jerome Gorin/Getty Images, 42; © Pongasn68/iStock.com, 44 top; Ray Hennessy/Unsplash, 25 row 4 right, 105; © Robby Gelbrich/EyeEm/Getty Images, 3; © robertharding/Alamy Stock Photo, 70; Savs/Unsplash, 67; Shaquon Gibson/Unsplash, 94; © steele2123/iStock.com, 117; © Stephen Simpson/Getty Images, 10; © Steve Satushek/Getty Images, 79; © StreetFlash/iStock.com, Exploration titles 58, 66, 72; © Supercaliphotolistic/iStock.com, 99 (hawk); © t_kimura/iStock.com, Exploration titles 36, 41, 48; © Thankful Photography/iStock.com, 49; © ullstein bild/Getty Images, 25 row 4 left; © Valeria Vechterova/iStock.com, 76; © wkunst/iStock.com, 44 middle; © Yanik Chauvin/stock.adobe.com, 112

ILLUSTRATIONS BY © Katie Vernon/Lilla Rogers Studio, except Devin Franklin, 29; © Elayne Sears, scat 74 & 75; Ilona Sherratt, 62, tracks 74 & 75, 133; Violet Corral, 26; Xavi Velázquez, 119

LETTERING THROUGHOUT BY Alethea Morrison

To my parents,
who have offered their unwavering support to me
and my work throught the years:

JAY DENNY FRANKLIN, whose exciting childhood stories
about his backyard exploration beckoned me outside to
create my own stories,

and **PATRICIA FARRELL FRANKLIN**, who taught me to
"waste not" — whether it be through recycling bottles,
appreciating spring peeper symphonies, or using the gifts
hidden inside my own heart.

CONTENTS

Your Wild Backyard, 6

1 Discovering a New Backyard, 11

2 Your Backyard Trees, 33

3 Your Backyard Mammals, 55

4 Your Backyard Birds, 81

5 Your Backyard Community, 107

Your Wild Backyard

In this book I use the word *back-yard* to describe a place in nature that you or I come to know very well — maybe better than any other human being! This can be the woods, a city park, a suburban backyard, or an empty lot.

We learn about it by sitting quietly, watching and hearing what goes on, noticing what birds and animals are doing, wandering around its different mini-areas, and observing its changes. Every day my own backyard grows more and more interesting as I learn its secrets.

I'll share my ways with you so you can discover a new backyard, too — and I'll begin by introducing my own teacher, Lenny Brown.

IT'S TIME FOR AN ADVENTURE!

As a boy living in the countryside, Lenny simply couldn't be kept indoors. He loved squishing barefoot through the beaver swamps in his backyard. When he grew up, Lenny and his wife, Deborah, founded Flying Deer Nature Center — a place where kids come to dig their toes into grassy fields, watch wiggling caterpillars, sneak through the forest, and spy on fuzzy fox kits as they play near their den.

Kids always come home from Flying Deer with an exciting tale to tell. The book you're holding brings this kind of fun right to your doorstep, and gets you adventuring outdoors and creating some of your own exciting nature stories to share.

Put On Your Owl Eyes is sprinkled with fascinating backyard stories written by Flying Deer staff, all of whom have spent years closely observing and investigating the natural world. You'll notice that each story's author has a "nature nickname" — something you, too, can have as you take this journey with us!

FIND YOUR NATURE NICKNAME

Nature nicknames link us in a fun way with our wilder backyard relatives. Mine is Green Frog. Green frogs and I both prefer to dress in green, enjoy sitting still, and love jumping into water! Here's how to find your own nickname:

1. *Have someone pick a name for you,* since a given nickname is better than a chosen one. Or ask them to write a few names on slips of paper and let you pick one from a hat.

2. *Keep it local.* Choose only wildlife that lives in your part of the country.

3. *Trust the magic.* Be open to what your name has to teach you. Do some research and keep your name at least until you reach the end of this book.

THE CORE ROUTINES OF NATURE CONNECTION

Have you ever played a game of hide-and-seek that lasted for hours, or even days? When my teacher, Jon Young, was about ten years old, he played one game that lasted for years! Jon was the seeker, and the hider was a sneaky red fox that lived in his backyard.

Again and again, Jon tried to catch a glimpse of this beautiful wild animal with its fluffy orange coat, golden eyes, and glistening black nose, but that red fox always slipped away unseen. In the end, early one morning at sunrise, Jon won the game. But it took many backyard visits and some help from his neighborhood mentor, Tom Brown, Jr.

Tom, a master tracker, had spent his whole life exploring, studying, and even living in the woods. Over ten years he taught Jon useful tricks, called Core Routines of Nature Connection, to help him find that wily back-yard fox, and in time Jon became a master tracker, too.

These Core Routines included **Fox Walking** — a stealthy way

SAFETY TIPS

Make sure your chosen backyard is safe! Get permission from the landowner, as well as permission from your supervising adult. Then research with an adult any possible natural hazards, which may include:
- Venomous snakes
- Ticks, venomous spiders, and dangerous insects
- Poisonous-to-touch plants
- Protective or ill mammals
- Severe weather
- Getting lost
- Widow-makers (dead trees that are ready to fall)

You'll most likely find that these hazards are less common than we think!

of moving through the landscape; listening for **Bird Language** — a way of studying birds to find hidden predators; and **Owl Eyes** — a way of seeing that can detect tiny movements, such as a fox's eye blinking in the bushes!

The fifteen Core Routines presented in this book will help you to discover the secretive wild residents (maybe even a wily fox!) of your own backyard.

Using This Book

You'll write notes, draw maps, and make sketches as you use this book. Find a notebook you like and keep it ready! And look for field guides in your public library. They are awesome resources stuffed with cool facts about our neighbors in nature.

Take the Backyard Quiz on page 132 before you start this book and again when you finish!

A "backyard" might be your own yard, a forest, a desert, a public green space, or a single tree growing on a street corner.

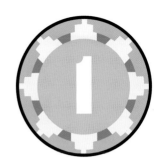

Discovering a New Backyard

This chapter introduces three Core Routines that will help you slow down and open your awareness to your backyard.

IN EXPLORATION 1, you will choose a **Sit Spot,** a special place you can visit each day to make observations.

IN EXPLORATION 2, you will be **Wandering** to explore part of your backyard in an entirely new way.

IN EXPLORATION 3, you will use **Mapping** to identify the habitats in your backyard and study them. Together, these Core Routines will open your eyes to *a bigger backyard.*

Tree Stinger

The sounds of afternoon traffic filled the air as I walked through a busy maze of city streets. Taking my usual route home, I cut through a small park with its grassy areas and a few old trees.

Suddenly I felt an urge to sit under one of the trees. Soon I was leaning against the gray, wrinkled trunk of a box elder, letting out a deep sigh, and beginning to take in my surroundings.

Immediately I spotted something glittering in the air before me. My eyes focused on a huge wasp with a body as long as my smallest finger, flying right at me. Behind it draped a thin black stinger so long it could have jabbed into my forearm and poked out the other side.

My heart pounded as this enormous insect landed on the very tree I was leaning against! It crawled over the tree's thickly furrowed bark, probing the crevices with its jittery antennae.

Then it stopped, sensing something I couldn't see. To my astonishment, it perched delicately on its six long, jointed legs, arched its brown and yellow hind parts, and began moving its three-inch-long, needle-like stinger as if about to sting the tree!

I lost all fear as I studied this creature that was more interested in the tree's bark than in me. It placed the tip of its stinger on the bark like a drill bit and then drove it deep into the trunk. A few minutes later, it withdrew its stinger and flew away.

Completely amazed, I hurried home and pulled my field guide off the shelf. Flipping through the pages, I found it: a drawing of a large wasp stinging a tree's bark. It was an ichneumon wasp, and what I thought was its stinger was actually an egg-laying apparatus!

I learned that I had just watched a female wasp use her antennae to detect a single grub deep inside the box elder tree. She then used her long, needle-like egg-laying apparatus to pierce the bark and lay a single parasitic egg on the grub's soft body.

Reading this I realized that if I had hurried through the park as usual that day, I would have completely missed the ichneumon and her egg-laying ritual. How many other creatures were quietly living their lives, unnoticed, within plain sight of the path I walked every day?

From then on, whenever I passed through the city park, I paid a visit to the box elder tree, which I renamed the Ichneumon Tree. Leaning against its trunk, I would take a deep breath, relax, and try to notice something I had never noticed before. Sometimes I wandered around, discovering unexpected surprises. **Soon, a place that had once seemed tame and empty had become a wild habitat where animals of countless forms slinked, slithered, and soared.**

The park became a place where I could endlessly make discoveries and connect with our great, wild earth. My eyes were now opened to a bigger backyard.

— *Devin (Green Frog)*

A FURRY HELLO

My first time finding a Sit Spot, I chose a small hemlock tree at the edge of a clearing in the woods. I sat down and said to myself, "Okay, for one hour I am going to sit still and observe my surroundings."

I sat as still as I could — watching and waiting. Wasn't I supposed to see some birds or something? Or maybe a fox? At least some bugs?!

I sat and sat for what seemed like an eternity. I figured that thirty minutes must have passed by. I peeked at my watch and saw that it was only three minutes. Three minutes!

"Oh boy," I thought. "I don't know if I can do this." But I practiced Sit Spot, day after day, and soon grew to love sitting very still and watching things happen in the landscape around me.

One day, I'd been sitting still for many minutes at my Sit Spot when a rabbit hopped out of the forest into the clearing. It watched me carefully for a while. Then it seemed to sense that I was not a threat and hopped toward me.

I sat stock still as it crept closer and closer. I felt its soft fur brush against the back of my hand. I could hardly breathe. Then it must have realized that I was a warm being — not a tree or a rock — and it hurried on its way.

My encounter with the rabbit made me feel I was part of the woods too, like I belonged there. It was a beautiful feeling. I decided to make my Sit Spot an important part of my life.

MICHELLE APLAND (Dandelion)

CHOOSE A SIT SPOT

A Sit Spot is a special area that you choose outdoors. Have a seat, settle in, and watch the world around you. It is a place all your own.

Your Sit Spot area can be under an old tree in the forest, at a bend in a stream, on a park bench, or on your own front stoop. Choose a place . . .

- that is easy to visit
- with a view of something wild
- with an appealing place to sit
- where you will enjoy spending time.

- A watch or other timepiece

WHAT TO DO

1. *Explore your backyard.* Take a leisurely walk around the area. Enjoy your surroundings, and notice any areas that might feel good to make your Sit Spot.

2. *Choose one spot* to be your Sit Spot area for your observations and explorations.

3. *Observe your backyard* quietly for at least ten minutes. What do you notice? Use all of your senses to observe your surroundings.

When you go indoors, write in your journal any observations you remember about your backyard — what you saw, heard, smelled, or felt while enjoying your Sit Spot area. Be sure to include the date.

SIT SPOT ON-THE-GO

Sometime today, make time for a Sit Spot On-the-Go. Pick a familiar place or one that's new. Wherever you are, take a moment to settle in and tune in to your surroundings, just as you did earlier at your Sit Spot. What do you notice at your Sit Spot On-the-Go?

In this Exploration you practiced sitting still and noticing your surroundings. How did that feel? Each time you visit, you will notice more and see more deeply into the world around you. If you noticed new things today, write a bit in your journal about how it felt different from your normal everyday activities.

Spruce Grove

One December morning I grabbed a jacket, laced up my boots, and stepped outside. Leaving a trail of boot prints behind me in the snow, I was soon in the hickory forest that bordered my backyard. Before me an old spruce grove rose up like a great green palace, holding the rest of the world out and a hushed silence in.

Hoo-OO-oo-OOoo! A barred owl called, breaking the silent spell. Now I sensed sound and movement everywhere: the wind sighing and rocking the treetops; red squirrels dancing like flames along tree limbs; and black-capped chickadees tapping on dry twigs to find hibernating insects.

I stepped deeper into the forest. Wild turkey scratches pocked the clean, bright snow. Nearby, a string of eastern coyote tracks wound its way through the trees.

I followed the coyote's tracks until they crossed those of a white-tailed deer. The deer trail led me to a bubbling spring. The water's surface was a mirror, reflecting a tapestry of branches, needles, and sky.

Feeling like a tourist, entranced by the beauty of a foreign land, I wandered on, my steps muffled by the snow — and then stopped

midstride. In front of me was a wide stone wall. Curled up on its snowy top lay what looked like a large gray ball of fur.

A head rose from the fur. Its yellow eyes were wide with surprise and looked right at me. It was a coyote! It sprang into the air, landed on all fours on the other side of the wall, and was gone in a flash.

The forest was silent. I was electrified. The timeless power of Wandering had opened up a new world within my familiar backyard.

DEVIN (Green Frog)

BE A TOURIST
IN YOUR OWN BACKYARD

When you are a tourist, you wander around with curiosity and excitement. Everything looks new: buildings, streets, trees. Wandering in a *familiar* place means exploring the landscape as a tourist would — full of wonder, enjoying your surroundings, open to whatever you find. To wander a landscape is to explore it without worrying about time, a goal, or a destination.

Think of a place in your own backyard that you have never truly explored. It might be an overgrown area you have never stopped to investigate, or a shrub you have passed by a hundred times but have never peeked inside. In this Exploration you will wander through your backyard, letting your curiosity guide you. Who knows what you'll find!

WHAT TO DO

1. **Visit your Sit Spot,** get comfortable, be quiet, and notice two or three familiar things.

2. **Now observe the way a tourist would** and notice two or three new things you have never noticed before.

3. **Survey your backyard** from your Sit Spot, notice which areas you're curious about, *and choose the place you will Wander today.*

4. **Have a Wander!** Your only goal is to discover what is there.

A TOURIST'S CURIOSITY

Sometime today, when you find yourself in a familiar place, stop what you are doing and pretend you are a tourist. Look around you. Choose something to look at — a soccer field, a flower garden, a mailbox, or even a person's face.

Now gaze at it the way a curious tourist might, as if you have never seen anything like it. Notice something about it you have never noticed before.

REFLECTIONS

Today you took time to Wander — to explore places and things — without any goal. Did Wandering affect how you saw these places and things? If so, how would you describe that? Write about it in your journal.

MAPPING MY KINGDOM

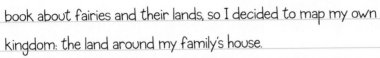

When I was ten I made a map of my backyard. I had just read a book about fairies and their lands, so I decided to map my own kingdom: the land around my family's house.

I made up my own names for each of the different regions, such as "The Dark and Wet Place," "The Dry and Warm Place," and "The Place to Watch Out for Ticks." **One region marked the magical spot where I once saw a white-tailed deer and stood a while as we watched each other.**

On my map there were roots that looked like feet and fallen trees that looked like sleeping people. I made note of all the animal homes that I had come across, like bird nests and groundhog holes. And of course I included the stream that trickled along the road and snaked through our yard, which secretly transported snapping turtles and frogs in its mysterious waters. I jotted down the four directions: north, south, east, and west.

Last of all, there in the bottom left-hand corner of my map, I put my family's house! When I was finished, I had a beautiful record of all the experiences I ever had in my backyard "kingdom."

IRENE LEE (Oriole)

WHAT'S A HABITAT?

Like any living creature, a skunk cabbage plant cannot survive in every type of place. For example, you will never find one growing on a dry, rocky ridgetop. It thrives in wet lowland areas, such as marshes, flooded stream banks, and wooded swamps. The type of place in which a specific kind of living creature can be found is called its *habitat*.

When you look at your backyard as a whole, habitats are the areas that look clearly different from one another. For example, if your backyard has a lawn with a line of trees growing at the edge, you can consider the lawn and the trees at the edge of the lawn to be two different habitats. What you name the habitats found in your backyard is up to you.

Here is a list of various habitats. Use it to identify and describe your backyard's habitats, or make up your own names.

COMMON HABITATS

FOREST
A wooded area dominated by trees.

THICKET
A brushy area dominated by wild shrubs and/or young trees.

FIELD
An open area dominated by grasses, weeds, and other wild-growing plants. Fields remain fields by being mown annually or grazed by animals.

HEDGEROW
A line of dense bushes and/or small trees that form a natural border. Hedgerows often grow at the edges of lawns and fields.

GARDEN OR FARM
A place where people cultivate crops, vegetables, and/or flowers.

LAWN
An open area, often surrounding a building or home, kept mown for appearance or for recreational purposes.

EXPOSED EARTH
Any small or large area where the soil is showing. This might be due to human activity such as plowing, burning, or construction.

URBAN LOT
A city space that was once developed but has no buildings on it now.

ROADS AND PATHWAYS
Routes that are kept clear for easier walking or driving.

WETLAND
Any area containing open water — ponds, lakes, or even puddles; also places with water-saturated soil, such as marshes, bogs, and soggy patches of lawn.

MAKE A
HABITAT MAP

Today you will explore your backyard and notice its habitats, then create a simple map of your backyard from memory. Give each habitat a name that feels right to you, which can be from the list or one you make up.

For example, if the area you have chosen as your backyard is in a city park, your habitats might be named *picnic area*, *playground*, *stream*, and so forth. If an area stands out because it looks different from its surroundings, call it a separate habitat.

WHAT TO DO

1. *Go to your Sit Spot and look out into your backyard.* What different habitats can you see from there? Give each its own name and list three or four on a page of your journal.

2. *Are there still more habitats* in your backyard? *Wander and find them!* Give each habit its own name and add it to your list.

3. *Choose your favorite habitat.* What sets it apart from the others around it?

4. *Draw a map of your backyard.* Mark your Sit Spot with an X. Add your Wandering place and any notable features (such as a tree, path, or building).

5. *Write the names* of the backyard habitats you've found at the heart of each area. Your map is complete!

HABITAT MATCH

As you go about your day, visiting a friend or riding on the bus, you may notice habitats all around you in a new way. Some may remind you of those in your backyard, while others may look completely different.

Earlier, you chose one backyard habitat as your "favorite." Do you think you'll encounter *that* kind today? Keep your eyes open to find a habitat that closely matches your favorite backyard habitat and notice one or two ways that they are similar. *Have fun!*

REFLECTIONS

Did the experience of Mapping today change how you look at your surroundings? How?

THE SWAMP

I once lived in a tiny cabin in the woods near Flying Deer Nature Center. Nearby was a small wetland I called the Swamp. It was only a five-minute walk from my cabin, but entering its soggy domain was like visiting a different planet, a place I might have read about in a science fiction novel.

Down in the belly of the Swamp where the black muck oozed, massive skunk cabbages grew like giant man-eating plants. A stream sliced through the center of the Swamp, its clear waters creeping mysteriously through a long tunnel of multiflora rose bushes hovering like hulking monsters with thorn-covered tentacles.

To its north, the Swamp was bordered by a berm of dry land, from which grew crooked black locust trees that looked like they might snatch up visitors by the collar and play with them in their gnarled fingers. This was a new landscape for me, and I loved it.

On my first day exploring, I chose a scraggly buckthorn tree in a small clearing by the stream as my Sit Spot. I visited the Swamp every day, roaming its various landscapes, then returned to my cabin after my Wanderings to draw a simple map of the terrain.

Every day after making a map I'd return to my Sit Spot and see the Swamp more deeply. I noticed patterns. The plants and trees weren't growing just anywhere, but only in certain areas. Skunk cabbage patches, for example, lived in soggy soils. Black locust patches grew only on dry land. **I began to see the Swamp as a jigsaw puzzle, each interlocking piece representing a small but unique habitat.**

    After two years of visiting this Sit Spot and drawing countless maps, I found that I knew and loved this place unlike any I had known or loved before. It was as though part of me had been laid into its fields of skunk cabbage, sucked gently into the black muck, and lodged inside the bedrock beneath the swamp. Looking back, I know this feeling arose from knowing the land more closely through Mapping.

DEVIN (Green Frog)

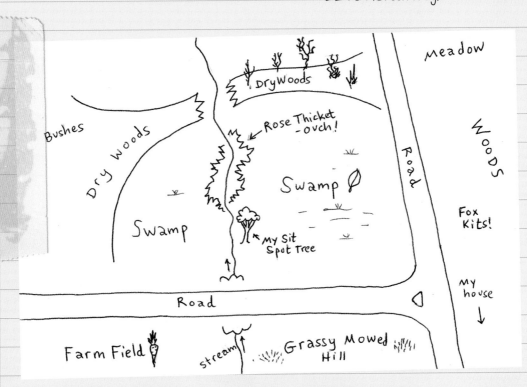

The Solace of Sit Spot

Ever since I was a little girl, whenever I was sad or upset I went to my backyard Sit Spot. Countless times, I sat in my little nook in the rock surrounded by trees, just breathing and feeling my body relax. I watched the creatures there and learned how diligent and tireless ants are, and how delicate a spider's work is. I watched in silence as chipmunks chattered at each other, woodpeckers knocked frantically on trees, and sparrows "alarmed" if a house cat was in the area.

Being a ten-year-old with an older brother and plenty of adults to misunderstand me was tough at times, but **my Sit Spot reminded me that nature offers solace to anyone, at any time, no matter the circumstances.** My Sit Spot accepted me in any mood, never judged me, and always left me feeling lighter and wiser than before.

— *Rabea Fuchshofen (Porcupine)*

YOUR BIGGER BACKYARD

This chapter offered some ways to learn about nature and see your backyard — wherever that may be — as *a new backyard*. You chose a special place in your backyard to become your very own Sit Spot, you followed your curiosity on a backyard Wander, and you Mapped some of the habitats you found there.

What did these adventures reveal about your backyard, and how have these practices helped you to discover a "bigger backyard"? Write your thoughts in your journal.

Your Backyard Trees

Did you ever look at a forest and find you couldn't identify the particular trees right in front of you? It's just a Wall of Green. We modern humans often perceive the natural world around us in a hazy, undetailed way. This is a starting point for learning and growth.

Chapter 2 presents three Core Routines to help untangle the Wall of Green that may stand in your own backyard.

EXPLORATION 4 helps you **Expand Your Senses,** paying conscious attention to information in the landscape, such as patterns of shape and texture.

EXPLORATION 5 sharpens your power to **Explore Field Guides** and learn more detail about your backyard trees.

EXPLORATION 6 is an adventure in **Mind's Eye Imagining,** using visual memory to integrate and recall information about your backyard trees.

Maple Palace

It was summertime, and I stood with Michelle in a dense copse of trees lovingly referred to in our neighborhood as the Maple Palace. Over the years, I had spent countless hours wandering through its tight labyrinth of narrow gray trunks and climbing high into its canopy of palmlike leaves.

Michelle held one of the tree's broad leaves out to me and asked if I had ever heard of a Norway maple. I had not. She pointed out the long and narrow leaf stem and the seven arrow-straight veins shooting out from the base of the leaf, each in a different direction. Other maples usually have five, she said.

I gazed up with new eyes at the maple palace and its green, cloudlike foliage. Yet, searching the landscape for another Norway maple, I couldn't find one. I could see maple trees, but that was all. This was the first time someone had taught me how to identify a specific *kind* of maple. Till then I had seen the forest as an indistinguishable Wall of Green.

Starting that day, whenever I spotted a maple leaf, I'd pick it up and scrutinize its margin, stem, and veins. I'd mentally compare it to other maple leaves. Sometimes I'd even take it home and sketch it, or look it up in a field guide.

After a few years, I no longer needed a leaf in my hand to identify the Norway maple. In mid-November, when all the other trees' leaves had fallen, its ripe-banana-colored foliage shouted out in the prewinter drabness. In early February, its gray, finely cracked bark was unique, and its stout, straight twigs clicked and clacked loudly in bitter winds. In late April, its flowers' intoxicating fragrance flooded the air like a rare perfume. And July's rains hitting its leaves sounded like the clapping of a thousand tiny hands.

One summer morning, riding in a car with Michelle, I gazed at the river of foliage flowing by my open window. Soon I realized I was counting the Norway maples we passed — *and I was up to seven.* **A tree that was once a stranger was now a beloved comrade waving at me from a crowd.** I had found a friend in what was once a Wall of Green.
— *Devin (Green Frog)*

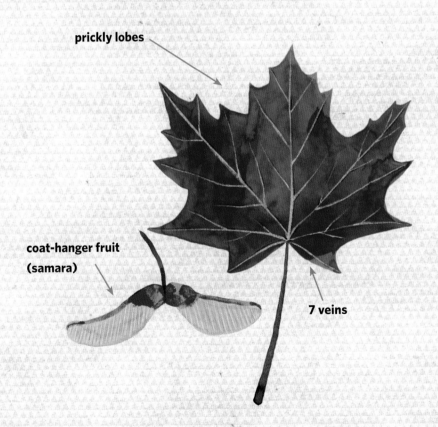

prickly lobes

coat-hanger fruit
(samara)

7 veins

EXPANDING THE SENSES

Whenever I settle into a new city, the first thing I do is find the wild places near my home. I might wander through a large park, or observe the natural space created by a single tree.

When I find a place that especially draws my attention, I open my senses and soak up all the sensations — cool air that has just been inhaled and exhaled by the leaves; a Jurassic landscape smothered by ivy vines and pierced by enormous western red cedar trees; or the mourning dove's soothing, lonely call.

Opening my senses to nature *in* the city helps me see the nature *of* the city. **When I watch office buildings breathing their workers in and out, I see a beehive.** When I watch people leaving home every day to collect what they need for their families, I see beavers fastidiously building lodges and squirrels gathering nuts for the long winter.

Soaking my senses in the city's wild places also helps me recognize the wildness in myself. I see my reflection in the dew on grass, in the bark of a warped locust tree, and in the scent of cedar, just as clearly as in the window of a store.

EMMA POST (Maple)

BEHOLD A TREE

To behold something is to meet it with all of your senses. **Expanding the Senses** is a Core Routine that enhances our ability to notice the unique sights, sounds, smells, and other information present in our backyard landscape.

BEFORE YOU BEGIN

In this activity you will choose a special tree to explore with your senses of sight, hearing, touch, and smell. Remember to be safe when exploring this tree, as some tree and shrub species contain toxins or prickers that can itch or that can poke.

    If your backyard does not include a tree, explore a shrub instead.

WHAT TO DO

1. *Walk to your Sit Spot,* settle in, then look around at your backyard. Can you see trees from where you sit? Spend a minute or two studying any you can see from your Sit Spot.

2. *Choose a tree.* Wander your backyard in search of a tree that you would like to safely explore with your senses.

3. *Use your senses* of sight, hearing, touch, and smell to investigate your tree. What colors, shapes, textures, and patterns can you see? Is this tree making any sounds on its own? What noises does it make as you run your hands over its bark, roots, and leaves? How would you describe the textures of the bark, leaves, and any other parts you can reach? How would you describe its scents?

FIVE PLANTS **NOT** TO TOUCH

If you are not sure whether you should touch your tree or the plants growing near it, look it up in a field guide or ask someone to help you identify them. Here are five hands-off plants to know.

poison ivy

poison oak

poison sumac

cow parsnip

stinging nettle

ONE-MINUTE SPONGE

Have you ever noticed what happens when you drop a dry sponge in water? Within seconds, the once-shriveled sponge swells up, eagerly absorbing its surroundings and growing to its full size. *Imagine how good that could feel!*

At some point today when you are feeling extra-comfortable, become like a dry sponge dropped into water. Wherever you are, use your senses to soak in the sights, scents, textures, and other aspects of your surroundings. If you were a dry sponge, and your surroundings were like water, what would you absorb? Let yourself be filled with these sensations for about a minute.

REFLECTIONS

Today you practiced Expanding the Senses. Were you able, at times in your day, to fully immerse yourself in your senses? If so, write in your journal about what that was like.

EXPLORING FIELD GUIDES

One early-autumn morning, I was leading a group of home-schooled children up a steep slope in a southern Appalachian forest. As we gathered for lunch, a sapling growing out of a gray, cracked stump at the edge of the clearing caught my attention.

Less than three feet in height, its leaves were long and sharply toothed, much like an American beech's, yet longer and a bit narrower. This sapling was different from the rest of the trees in this forest, all of which I knew very well.

Out of nowhere, the word "chestnut" popped into my mind. I'd seen pictures of American chestnut trees but I had never met one in the field. That species once dominated the forests of the Appalachian Mountains. They were huge, abundant, and important, and among other things they provided vital natural ladders for many creatures, including humans.

We looked in a tree field guide. We compared the descriptions of similar trees and found that the length of the leaves proved our tree to be an American chestnut! **We all felt joyful that our new camp was blessed by this ancestor tree.**

Later on the area's most respected naturalist confirmed our hypothesis. We were proud to have found a wild American chestnut — a powerful symbol of healing, renewal, and hope — in our backyard forest!

KEVIN BOSE (Hazelnut)

MEET A
NEW NEIGHBOR

Today you will explore your backyard to find a New Neighbor (in this case a tree) whose name you do not yet know. This could be your Sit Spot, your Beholding Tree, or another tree that strikes your curiosity.

You will get to know this New Neighbor tree by observing its bark, twigs, leaves (if it has any), and any other notable features you see. Then you will document your observations. Finally, you will dive into your field guide, using your leaf and twig observations to help you find your way.

BEFORE YOU BEGIN

The outdoor portion of today's activity will take a little more time than the previous activities did.

WHAT TO DO

1. *Relax into your Sit Spot* and notice all the trees in your backyard *whose names you do not know*. Choose a tree that interests you.

2. *Pluck a leaf* from your New Neighbor tree, and sketch it in your journal. (You can tape the leaf on the same page.) If there are no leaves, find a twig *on the tree*, look for buds arranged along its length, and then sketch what you see.

3. *Sketch another interesting part* of your tree, such as its bark, fruit, nut, seed, or flower.

GETTING TO KNOW A LEAF

Now examine your leaf closely. Your careful observations will help you when you are ready to explore a field guide.

Is the leaf broad and flat or narrow and needle-like?

Write the answer in your journal.

My leaf is a **broadleaf**.

A broadleaf is flat and wide, like these maple leaves.

My leaf is a **needle leaf**.

A needle leaf is needle-shaped — long and narrow, like these spruce leaves.

Is the leaf entire, lobed, or toothed?

These words describe the leaf's edges. Are the edges smooth, serrated like a saw blade, or lobed like fingers? Write the answer in your journal.

Mine is an **entire** leaf.

An entire leaf has smooth edges, like this magnolia leaf.

Mine is a **toothed** leaf.

A toothed leaf has serrated margins, like these birch leaves.

My leaf is **lobed.**

A lobed leaf has margins that resemble a jigsaw puzzle piece with sinuses (indentations) and lobes (large fingerlike or spikelike projections). This oak leaf is lobed.

Leaf edges can be both lobed and toothed, like the maple leaves on the previous page.

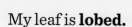

Is the leaf simple or divided?

Write the answer in your journal.

My leaf is **simple.**

A simple leaf is just one single leaf, like this oak leaf.

My leaf is **divided.**

A divided leaf has a central leaf stem with miniature "leaves" (called leaflets) growing out of it, like this ash leaf.

Note: Did you write that your leaf is "simple"? Beware! Beginners often trick themselves with this one because they don't know the difference between a leaf stem and a twig.

A *twig* is a woody part of the tree's structure; a twig doesn't die and drop from the tree like a leaf does. The *leaf stem* of a divided leaf often looks like a twig but it isn't, because every year it dies and drops from the tree, along with the rest of the leaf.

When you plucked your leaf from the tree, was it a simple leaf growing out of a woody twig, or did you actually pluck a leaflet off the soft leaf stem of a larger divided leaf?

The Fun of a Field Guide

Whenever I explore a field guide, it reminds me of exploring my backyard. I Wander freely from page to page, encountering wonderful new sights and sometimes making delightful discoveries.

As you explore your own guide, put your curiosity in charge. Do you see something that strikes you as odd or fantastic? Investigate it. Give yourself ample time to explore in this way and you're guaranteed to make some exciting discoveries!

As you search for your tree, use your leaf/twig observations as a guide. For example, if your leaf is lobed and toothed, pay special attention in your book to any tree with lobed, toothed leaves. If you wish, write any guesses about the species of your New Neighbor tree in your journal.

GAME OF THE DAY

CHANCE ENCOUNTER

Imagine you've recently moved into a new neighborhood and met a new (human!) neighbor. Later, you are walking down a crowded sidewalk across town when a familiar face flashes past you. You think it might be your new neighbor!

You double back to find out. You call their name, they turn around and . . . it *is* your new neighbor. What a chance encounter!

Today, stay alert to the fact that your New Neighbor tree could be growing where you don't expect to find it. If a tree catches your attention, spend a few minutes checking it out. Study its twigs, buds, bark and leaves. Is it your New Neighbor tree, or a different kind?

REFLECTIONS

Today you explored a field guide and met a New Neighbor. Did you learn something new today about how field guides can help backyard learning? Write some of your thoughts in your journal.

EAGLE

MIND'S EYE IMAGINING

It is a cloudless day and you and I are eagles, soaring side by side, a mile above your backyard. Observe the terrain stretching in all directions beneath us. Is it flat and smooth, or wrinkled with mountains, hills, and valleys? Can you see forests, or is the landscape bare? Or is it a cityscape of tall buildings, roads, and waterways?

Close your eyes and imagine flying one mile above the earth. Look for the forest closest to your backyard. What does it look like from up here?

Now let's fly even higher – higher than even an eagle could possibly fly – so high that we can view the entire North American continent in a single glance! As we gaze down upon our continent encircled by vast waters, see how your local forest fits into the larger network of forests found on the landmass we call North America. Spend a few moments imagining this.

It's time to head home. **Let's fold our wings behind us and dive-bomb down to your backyard.** Feel the wind ripping past as we plummet closer and closer to earth! Individual trees are starting to become visible. We stretch our wings and flap them mightily, landing gracefully at the top of your New Neighbor tree.

What do things look like from here? Close your eyes and take a few minutes to study your backyard from this treetop.

DEVIN (Green Frog)

TAKE A
FOREST SOAR

The Core Routine of **Mind's Eye Imagining** means visualizing something we cannot physically see from where we are. For example, we just imagined we were eagles flying high above the earth; you could also remember an image from a dream. Now it's time to give Mind's Eye Imagining a try in your own backyard.

WHAT TO DO

1. *Visit your Sit Spot,* settle in, and close your eyes. When you feel relaxed, imagine that you are sitting on top of your New Neighbor tree. What does your backyard look like from there? What can you see in each direction?

2. *Visit your New Neighbor tree* and stand against it. Now study your backyard with your actual eyes. What new things do you notice about your backyard from that point of view?

3. *Draw a map of your backyard,* starting with your New Neighbor tree. Include any features that stand out in your memory: buildings, trees, footpaths, and anything else you remember seeing from your New Neighbor tree.

IMAGINING YOUR SIT SPOT

Tonight as you lie in bed, before falling asleep, imagine you are at your Sit Spot. Using Mind's Eye Imagining, observe your backyard from the perspective of your Sit Spot. How many details about your backyard can you notice using your Mind's Eye? In your imagination, what can you smell, feel, hear, and taste?

Enjoy imagining your Sit Spot for a few minutes before falling asleep. Maybe you'll dream about it tonight!

REFLECTIONS

Today you used Mind's Eye Imagining to Explore your backyard. What was it like? What did you notice about your backyard by using Mind's Eye Imagining? Write about it in your journal.

NIGHT FLIGHT

One cool summer night I was camping in
an old grove of American beech trees, and a
strong wind woke me up. As my eyes focused on the
crescent moon above, I remembered my dream . . .

I was flying through the great void of our solar system. **I rushed by
Saturn, nearly grazing its icy rings. I passed the crystal blue
jewel of Neptune.** Then I circled back toward the great fireball we call
the Sun, awakening with a jolt just before I would have been burned by
the flames leaping from its surface.

And here I was, lying under the great cosmos, listening to the wind —
now howling, now whispering — through the beech grove around me, here,
on Earth.

When morning came, I beheld my surroundings through new eyes.
The beech leaves rustled softly in the morning light. **I imagined our star,
the Sun, sending out a field of energy so immense that it rules
climates and weather systems on a planet 93 million miles away.**

I watched one particularly tall beech for a long while, listening intently
as its limbs creaked in a wind that came right out of my dream. Goose
bumps covered my body and a shiver ran through me as I realized just
how vast and mysterious this world is.

JAY LEAVITT (Kingfisher)

An Endless Journey

My dear friend Raphael came east for her first time to hike with me on Vermont's Long Trail. She loves nature, but she felt claustrophobic in Vermont's forests, with masses of unfamiliar trees and plants crowding the hiking trail like a blurry green tunnel. **Back home in the Southwest, she could identify nearly every living creature. But here, everything seemed woven into a uniform green fabric.**

As the days passed, Raphael noticed certain plants and trees recurring in the landscape. The more she studied the passing vegetation, the more plant patterns she began to recognize.

I helped her with the names. In time, the feathery, dark-green tree with short, flat, blunt-tipped needles became "eastern hemlock," and the feathery, dark-green tree with short, round, sharp-tipped needles became "black spruce."

By the end of the hike, Raphael saw not a blur of green but unique, individual plants and trees. For a naturalist, learning is a journey that never ends.

— *Michelle Apland (Dandelion)*

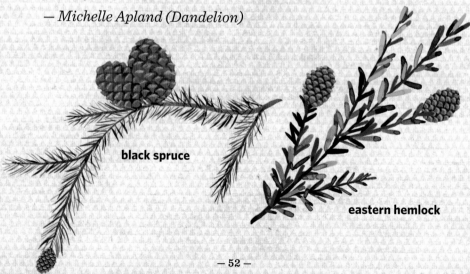

black spruce

eastern hemlock

THE WALL OF GREEN

In chapter 2, you learned about the *Wall of Green* — the limit of our knowledge and awareness of our natural surroundings — and learned three techniques for expanding those limits.

How have the Core Routines of **Expanding the Senses**, **Exploring Field Guides**, and **Mind's Eye Imagining** helped you expand the limits of your backyard awareness? Write your thoughts in your journal.

Your Backyard Mammals

Chapter 3 offers ways to find and observe animals in nature, using the Core Routines.

IN EXPLORATION 7, you will put on your **Fox Feet** and use the Fox Walk to move across the landscape and see your backyard the way a fox might.

IN EXPLORATION 8, you will visit a new planet and use **Questioning** to discover something new.

AND IN EXPLORATION 9, you will go **Tracking** to study the clues backyard critters leave behind.

So let's get started!

Icebound Stream

In the deep of winter, my breath hanging like a ghost in the air, I felt drawn to visit the stream that flowed through my Sit Spot. The cracking and crunching of my footsteps rang out in the stillness and I instinctively adjusted my pace, entering the slow, meditative gait of Fox Walking. As I walked in this way, my mind calmed and my senses opened.

A transparent skin of ice had grown over the gurgling waters of the stream. Underneath, large bubbles of light and dark danced in slow motion downstream, changing shape as they flowed.

As I gazed deeply, I noticed one of the dark bubbles moving *upstream*. Before I could imagine what might be traveling upstream in such icy waters, a small, furry, brown face poked out of a hole in the ice.

The little face glanced to its left, then to its right. Then a long, furry, snakelike body launched into the air and onto the ice, and four sets of claws clicked as it landed. The creature's glistening, dripping fur was chocolate brown. *It was a mink!*

Again this sleek aquatic weasel looked cautiously around, then it bounded upstream across the ice. Stopping in front of another hole in the surface, it glanced over its shoulder once more, then slipped into the hole and back into the frigid, flowing waters.

Visible through the clear ice, the long, dark, bubble-like shape swam steadily upstream. At a third hole, it repeated the whole sequence: *Poke head out, glance around, hop onto ice, glance around, bound to next hole,*

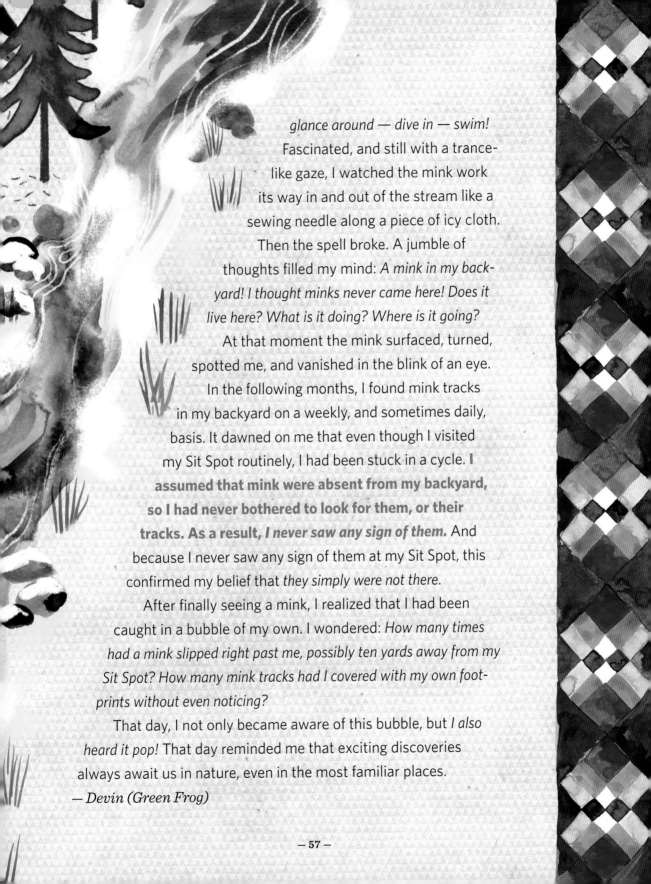

glance around — dive in — swim! Fascinated, and still with a trance-like gaze, I watched the mink work its way in and out of the stream like a sewing needle along a piece of icy cloth. Then the spell broke. A jumble of thoughts filled my mind: *A mink in my back-yard! I thought minks never came here! Does it live here? What is it doing? Where is it going?* At that moment the mink surfaced, turned, spotted me, and vanished in the blink of an eye. In the following months, I found mink tracks in my backyard on a weekly, and sometimes daily, basis. It dawned on me that even though I visited my Sit Spot routinely, I had been stuck in a cycle. **I assumed that mink were absent from my backyard, so I had never bothered to look for them, or their tracks. As a result, *I never saw any sign of them.*** And because I never saw any sign of them at my Sit Spot, this confirmed my belief that *they simply were not there.*

After finally seeing a mink, I realized that I had been caught in a bubble of my own. I wondered: *How many times had a mink slipped right past me, possibly ten yards away from my Sit Spot? How many mink tracks had I covered with my own foot-prints without even noticing?*

That day, I not only became aware of this bubble, but *I also heard it pop!* That day reminded me that exciting discoveries always await us in nature, even in the most familiar places.

— *Devin (Green Frog)*

STINKER
the
RED SQUIRReL

My first wilderness mentor, Dan Fisher, once showed me what happened when I entered the forest in a rush. Birds scattered and dove into the bushes, squirrels chattered from tree limbs, and deer bounded away, snorting. Then he showed me how to Fox Walk.

The smooth gait of the Fox Walk helped me slow down and "join" the flow of nature, rather than disturb it. I practiced Fox Walking everywhere (even in school) until I could walk through the forest without disturbing the birds or even the deer.

But one forest animal refused to ignore me: Stinker.

Red squirrels are supreme tattlers. Their alarm cries alert the forest that a human is approaching. Stinker was a particularly cantankerous red squirrel who lived near my Sit Spot. Every day, he chittered, twittered, chattered, trilled, screeched, and preached at my approach. His raucous alarms put everyone else on edge, and I could never see the wild turkeys, white-tailed deer, red fox, and eastern coyote that also lived there.

One day I was walking to my Sit Spot, an ancient sunken carriage road flanked by thickets of rose and honeysuckle, punctuated by the twisting trunks of black cherry trees and the stout trunks of bitternut hickories. Stinker eyed me from a hickory branch. I prepared to give him my customary scowl.

And then something happened: I relaxed.

All tension drained from me. I felt buoyant, happy, with no need to obsess about Stinker. As I Fox Walked peacefully, I gazed straight ahead and watched him from the corners of my eyes as I passed. He didn't make a single peep!

That day two white-tailed deer and a flock of wild turkeys came so close to my Sit Spot that I could see their eyelashes. From then on, Stinker let me walk in peace to my Sit Spot. Only when I was unable to relax completely did he ever have to remind me with his chitters, his twitters, and his chatters.

DEVIN (Green Frog)

PUT ON YOUR
FOX FEET

Have you ever watched a fox travel across the landscape? Whether in a casual trot or a full gallop, its movements are amazingly fluid.

The Fox Walk is modeled on the fox's graceful style. It allows humans to move through the natural world without frightening the animals around us.

WHAT TO DO

1. ***Stand up and place a pen or pencil lightly on top of your head.*** Don't let it fall off! Notice how your body helps: your back naturally wants to straighten (not hunch), your knees want to bend slightly (not lock straight), and your eyes want to gaze forward (not down).

2. ***Take a deep breath*** — in and out — without letting the pen fall off. Take another deep breath and, as you exhale, let your shoulders completely relax.

3. **Raise one foot** and pretend to take a step, but just before touching the ground hold it steady in the air.

4. **Now let your foot kiss the ground** like a gently falling feather, rather than slamming down. The Fox Walk is a smooth movement.

5. **Walk slowly.** If your pen clatters to the floor, adjust your *posture*, *relaxation,* and *smooth movement.* If this is too easy, adjust your pen to a more precarious position.

6. **Add your imagination.** As you Fox Walk, pretend that *you are a fox*, smoothly padding along on soft, slipperlike feet, swiveling your head from side to side, sniffing the air with your wet black nose and scanning the landscape with your large, furry, highly receptive ears. *You've got your Fox Feet on!*

This is the magic moment that separates Fox Walking from "normal" walking! Instead of letting your foot slam onto the ground, let it kiss the ground like a gently falling feather.

MEET THE RED FOX

Red foxes are renowned for their stealth and their adaptability. I've watched them creep through the forest and saunter down city sidewalks.

Let's find out if this mammal lives in your area by consulting the range maps below. On a range map, shaded areas show where a particular species lives.

Study the maps to pinpoint where *you* live. If your "pinpoint" is in the yellow-shaded red fox range, red foxes live in your area and possibly your backyard! If you live in the rust-shaded gray fox range, you have gray foxes instead. Maybe you have both species!

Let's learn more about the life and behaviors of the red fox, using your field guide. Here are some questions you might have:

- What do they eat?
- What time of day are they most active?
- Where (in what kinds of habitats) are they most commonly found?
- Look up *"Fox, red"* in your field guide's index, turn to the page indicated, and read everything in the guide about red foxes.

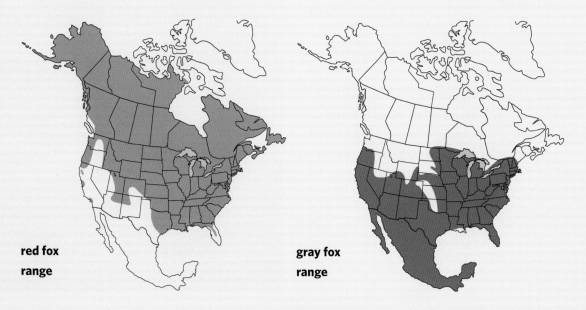

red fox range

gray fox range

SEARCH FOR FOX SPOTS

It's time to use your new knowledge to find *Fox Spots*: particular places that a fox might want to visit, while passing through your backyard.

WHAT TO DO

1. **Fox Walk to your Sit Spot.** Get comfortable and imagine you are a fox settling in.

2. **Observe your backyard** the way a fox might. What would be most interesting to a fox?

3. **Find a red fox feeding spot.** Using a slow Fox Walk, Wander your backyard to where a red fox could find food. When you find the right place, take a minute or two to investigate it.

4. **Find a red fox hiding spot.** Still using a Fox Walk, Wander your backyard to where you think a red fox would like to hide. Once you find a hiding place, take a minute or two to investigate it.

GO SLOWLY

Sometime while you are walking today, slow down and move in a Fox Walk. Use the same fluid, easy manner that you practiced earlier. Move at half of your normal pace.

At the same time, expand your senses and tune in to your surroundings. This is especially fun along a very familiar route.

REFLECTIONS

As you Fox Walked today, was there a moment when you noticed a shift in how you felt? How was that different from your normal everyday state of being? Write about it in your journal.

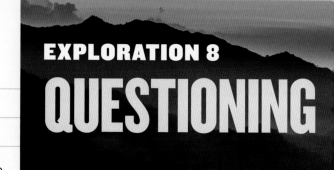

I was walking with my nephew through a park near his suburban Washington, D.C. home. It was a winter's evening, close to dusk, and the wizened, leafless oak and maple trees reached to the sky with thousands of outstretched branches. As we gazed at their silhouettes against the deep blue sky, **we noticed a strange, leafy mass about the size of a basketball wedged in the upper branches of one tree.**

"What is that?" my nephew asked. "A bird's nest?"

"Good question," I replied. "Let's find out!"

We explored and found many of these leaf balls throughout the park. Almost every tree had one, and some even had two!

Then a gray squirrel bounded across the grass and scurried up a tree trunk. Silhouetted against the dim glow of the twilight sky, it danced gracefully along the branches, leaped across space into another tree, descended the second tree's branches, then crept toward a leaf ball.

We watched, astonished, as the squirrel squeezed its body into the leaf ball! We looked at each other with enormous smiles.

My nephew was amazed because he had just witnessed — with his own eyes — the answer to his nature question, while also discovering something new about squirrels. I, too, was amazed because I had just witnessed **the power of questioning in action.**

DEVIN (Green Frog)

PONDER A
GRAY SQUIRREL

Questions create a bridge from the world of what we know to the world of what we do not yet know. Let's explore that bridge now.

WHAT TO DO

1. *Ponder what you already know about gray squirrels.* Come up with a simple fact about this animal, and write it in your journal. For example, in this Exploration's opening story, you can find a fact about squirrels' behavior (*they climb trees*) and a fact about their lives (*they sleep in leaf balls*). What else do you know about them?

2. *Wonder what you don't yet know about gray squirrels.* What else do you wonder about them? Think of a question and write it in your journal.

3. *Look up "Squirrel, gray" in your field guide.* Study whatever interests you about this animal. Open yourself to new knowledge. What new fact did you learn about gray squirrels?

ON PLANET Q

Have you heard the news? Astronomers recently discovered a new planet in our solar system! What is more shocking is that it — like planet Earth — contains numerous life forms! Some of its creatures are similar to those found on Earth, while others are completely different.

You have been selected for a solo mission. Your job will be to observe the planet's mammalian life, and report back to headquarters with your findings.

After ten days of interplanetary travel, you land safely on the new planet's surface. You step out through the research capsule's door and behold a new world filled with wonders.

As you start taking notes, however, you find that you can write only in the form of questions. A whole planet where you can only ask questions! Dedicated to your mission, you fill your research journal with questions about the mysterious and fascinating ways of the planet's mammalian life.

Some weeks later, your return to Earth is hailed with global excitement, and your observations are welcomed with scientific elation. Through your thoughtful and creative Questioning, much is learned about this new world.

But that is not all. Because you painted a picture of life on this planet only through questions, the public was hungry for more: more details, more information, and more knowledge!

In honor of your research and the many questions you brought back from the planet, the scientific community unanimously agrees to name the new world "Planet Q."

POSE A **QUESTION**

Just like on Planet Q, in this activity you will take a Wander through your backyard as though it were part of a new planet and ask questions about its mammalian life.

Ask silly questions: *How many hairs does that squirrel have on its tail?* Or serious questions: *Do any dangerous mammals live here, and how can I keep myself safe around them?*

Ask specific questions: *Where do the squirrels in my backyard sleep at night?* Or general questions: *How long have mammals existed on this planet?* As long as you're having fun, there are no wrong questions!

WHAT TO DO

1. ***Visit your Sit Spot and settle in.*** Gaze at your backyard through the eyes of a curious "mammologist." What questions come to mind about mammals and your backyard?

2. ***Visit your New Neighbor tree.*** What questions about mammals come to mind while looking at your tree?

3. ***Go to the Fox Spots*** you discovered earlier — the places where you think a fox might feed or hide — and ask some mammal questions about these places.

4. ***Wander the rest of your backyard*** and note as many mammal questions as you would like!

BURNING QUESTION

Have you ever thought up a question that not only made you curious, but *it consumed you with a desire to know the answer*? Have you ever wanted an answer so badly, you went to great lengths to find it? My teacher, Tom Brown, Jr., refers to this type of question as a *burning question*. You probably have a burning question, too. Write it down in your journal and see if you can find the answer.

REFLECTIONS

After asking questions today, do you feel more connected with your backyard? What specifically do you feel more connected to? Write your thoughts in your journal.

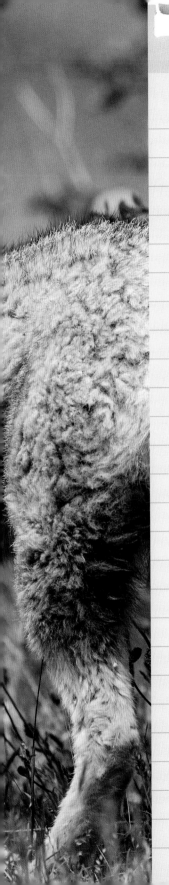

GRAY FOX

One spring morning I saw the body of a gray fox lying motionless on the side of the road. It was clearly dead. It was a female, with enlarged nipples as if she had been nursing a litter of pups.

A stream of questions entered my mind. In which months do gray foxes raise their young? If this is a nursing mother, how far away is her den, and in what direction? **How long ago was this fox killed? Are her pups still alive?**

If this was a nursing mother, I knew she would not have wandered too far from her pups. Scanning the landscape, I asked myself, "If I were a gray fox living here, where would I dig my den?"

A river was nearby, flowing past a small forested hill, with a field just beyond. Skirting the hill, I crossed the field to where a brushy, wooded slope eased its way down to the river. There, beneath the roots of an old stump, was a large hole with fresh, bright sand spilling out of it — **clearly an animal den of some sort.**

As I crept closer, I found the leg bone of a rabbit lying near the entrance, suggesting that this den indeed belonged to a fox. I looked for tiny fox prints or other signs of life, but found none. Another flood of questions rushed through my mind, but they would have to wait for another day. I had to be on my way.

DAN YACOBELLIS (Deer)

FOLLOWING CLUES

One snowy February day I came across a string of animal tracks in my backyard. My first question was: "Who left these tracks?"

The footprints looked like a child's, with a pair of tiny, five-toed prints in the front like a child's hands, and a pair of larger, more elongated prints in the back. A long, pointy claw had pressed into the snow at the tip of each toe. **These prints belonged to a raccoon!**

My next question: "When did the raccoon make these tracks?"

I looked closely. Each print was crisp and clean, while other tracks in the area were vague, blurred by weather and time. This trail was definitely fresh.

Next question: "What was the raccoon doing as it moved?"

As my eyes tracked its footprints, my Mind's Eye pictured its furry rump waddling through the snowy forest. I imagined it ambling along a thin trickling stream to a craterlike puddle and peering into its depths, whiskers twitching.

Then the tracks showed that it turned completely around to face the direction it came from — something had interrupted the raccoon's peaceful wandering! **Suddenly it had galloped away from this intruder — which I realized must have been me!**

Giving my ring-tailed neighbor some space, I sat for a moment and then continued tracking. I was relieved to see that, with time, the gait changed from a startled gallop to a relaxed walk.

The raccoon trail passed a cavelike hole at the base of a massive maple tree, and I peered inside. As my eyes adjusted to the shadowy, musty darkness, I made out a large ball of bristling, breathing . . . quills! A porcupine was crouched, facing in the opposite direction, just inches from my nose!

I quickly pulled out my head, pausing to admire the creature's backside, thick with quills. And I wondered — "**Did the raccoon lead me to this spot on purpose?** Did it make a special trip to this porcupine's tree as a little trap for me, its pursuer?"

I will never know for sure, but I went home delighted by the idea that this furry backyard neighbor might have been that clever.

DEVIN (Green Frog)

THE SIX ARTS OF TRACKING

All types of animals can leave noticeable tracks and sign on the landscape. The Core Routine of **Tracking** — finding, following, and interpreting the evidence left behind by wildlife — is a wonderful way to enter more deeply into the natural world around us.

Tracks vs. Sign

What's the difference between tracks and sign?

Tracks are footprints left by an animal.

Sign is any clue other than footprints left behind by an animal. Examples: anything that has been scraped, chewed, or rubbed by an animal, as well as *scat* (fecal material), and trails worn into the ground.

Six Doorways into the Animal World

The Core Routine of Tracking is based on asking questions. In the book *Animal Tracking Basics*, my teacher Jon Young presents the Six Arts of Tracking — six doorways into the world of Tracking. Each is represented by a question: *Who, What, When, Why, Where,* and *How.*

In this Exploration's opening story these questions helped identify the tracks left behind by a raccoon.

COYOTE

Tracks

front   rear

Scat

RED FOX

Tracks

front   rear

Scat

Who: Who left the sign?

For example: *Was it a mammal? Was it a canine? Was it my neighbor's dog?*

What: What did the animal do?

For example: *Was the animal sitting, walking, running, or doing something else? Did it spend a lot of time here? How did it move its body to leave this type of sign?*

When: When did the animal leave this track or sign?

For example: *Was this track or sign left behind an hour ago, a few weeks ago, or more than a month ago? How might sunlight, rain, or other weather factors have affected the appearance of this track?*

Why: Why did the animal do what it did?

For example: *Why did the animal leave this track or sign here instead of in a different place? Why was it here at this time of year, and at the time of day it passed through?*

Where: Where did the animal come from and where did it go from here?

For example: *Could I follow the tracks and sign left by the animal from here? If not, could I guess where it went? Where is the animal right now?*

How: How did the animal feel?

For example: *Did the animal feel comfortable? Startled? Hungry? Aggressive?*

RACCOON

Tracks

front rear

Scat

STRIPED SKUNK

Tracks

front rear

Scat

INVESTIGATE
TRACK AND SIGN

In this activity you will search for an interesting animal track or sign in your own backyard. The track or sign you choose can be from a mammal, bird, insect, amphibian, or any other living creature (except humans!).

1. *Visit your Sit Spot.* As you settle in, inspect your surroundings for any track or sign that may have been created by a member of your backyard community.

2. *Visit the biggest tree* in your backyard. What tracks or sign can be found near or on (or even inside) this tree? If you discover an interesting track (footprint) or sign (scrape, rub, chew, scat, and so on), compare it to the graphic on pages 74 and 75, and check your field guide.

3. *If you find no track or sign* at the tree, Wander your backyard until you find one, then compare it to the graphic and study it.

EYES OF A TRACKER

Sometime today, look for a track or sign in your ordinary environment. You do not have to go outside — tracks and sign are everywhere! They might include: a coat hanging on a hook by a door, the aromas of a meal being prepared, or the first sounds of your sister or brother waking in the morning.

Like animal footprints, any of these signs can offer a new doorway to a hidden world, when seen through the eyes of a tracker! Once you find a sign, investigate it by using some of the techniques of Tracking that you learned in this Exploration.

REFLECTIONS

Write a bit in your journal about what you saw through the eyes of a tracker.

Close Encounter

One morning in late April, I was exploring a wetland near my home, hoping to find a den. I spotted an old stump whose roots formed a large dark opening near its base. Slowly I Fox Walked, my eyes scanning the ground for tracks and sign, my ears attuned to every sound.

The stump was about ten feet away from me, at eye level. I took a few silent steps. All at once, the dark opening revealed itself to be the back of a sleeping black bear!

The bear turned and looked me straight in the eye. A cold wave of adrenaline surged through me from head to toe, and my body responded instinctively — averting my eyes, and smoothly backing away from the den. Thankfully, the bear never followed.

I had interrupted the bear's sleep and intruded on its privacy. In return, the bear had silently yet powerfully communicated its displeasure, refraining from teaching me a lesson of greater consequence.

I was struck by the gentleness and tolerance shown to me by this powerful animal. I would make sure to reciprocate the respect shown to me that day in any future interactions I might have with its kind.

— *Josh Wood (Barred Owl)*

OBSERVING MAMMALS

In this chapter, you have learned different skills that can be useful in expanding your awareness, especially your awareness of the lives of your backyard mammals. These skills included the Core Routines of Animal Forms (specifically, **Fox Walk**), **Questioning**, and **Tracking**.

How have these routines affected your awareness and understanding of your backyard animals? Write your thoughts in your journal.

Your Backyard Birds

For the creatures that inhabit our backyards, life is a matter of moment-to-moment survival. Chapter 4 presents three Core Routines that will help you see more deeply into the lives of your backyard birds.

IN EXPLORATION 10, you will put on your **Owl Eyes** to sharpen your peripheral vision and help you notice more of the birds that live in your backyard.

IN EXPLORATION 11, **Deer Ears** will help you hear sounds in nature, such as bird calls, and determine their exact location.

EXPLORATION 12 presents the core principles of **Bird Language** — the gossip network of nature that is always talking about things like Cooper's hawks, house cats . . . and you!

So open the curtains to the stage of your backyard — *let's journey into the exciting world of birds!*

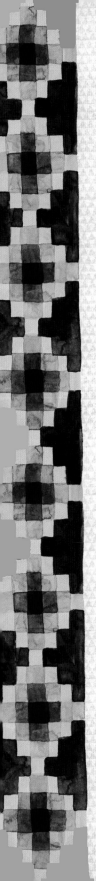

Incident by a Cedar Tree

On a gentle December evening, Michelle and I were walking through suburban Baltimore as dusk fell. A question arose: "Where do the birds sleep on a winter's night, in a place like this?" Very soon, we found an answer.

As we passed a yard where a lone cedar tree grew near the sidewalk, we heard an awful racket. Clearly, the tree's dense, protective greenery was a favorite roosting spot for a noisy flock of white-throated sparrows. Their shimmering banter filled the air as they jockeyed for prime positions, like too many children squeezing into a bed. We stopped to relish the sweet, jangly calls that filled the evening air.

As the last of the day's pale orange light drained out of the western sky, a mourning dove landed on one of the cedar tree's limbs, almost close enough for us to touch. It perched there, head cocked to one side, blinking at us with a curious, dubious expression. It circled around itself in place for a few seconds, like a dog preparing to bed down, but then stopped. It cocked its head in our direction once more, blinked, and flew noisily into the air, over the lawn, perhaps seeking a safer roost.

Seemingly out of nowhere, like a stray bullet, something crow-sized shot through the dusk air, colliding with the mourning dove and disappearing in an explosion of feathers. Every creature in the cedar tree fell silent. A cloud of feathers rocked gently back and forth in the dimming air.

Unable to resist our curiosity, Michelle and I crept closer in a quiet Fox Walking fashion. There we saw it — a Cooper's hawk, pinning the mourning dove to the grass with its sharp talons, yanking out breast feathers with its curved beak and tossing them into the air like a fountain. The hawk looked up, spotted us, and flapped off — clutching its dinner — into the dark of an adjacent backyard.

— *Devin (Green Frog)*

Shape Shifter

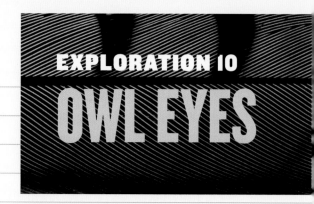
I had been sitting for many, many hours at my temporary Sit Spot. The mountaintop forest was peaceful and still, its branches filled with the fresh green leaves of June. I had yet to see any wildlife.

Looking up, I suddenly saw a huge wasps' nest hanging from a tree branch, only a few paces in front of me. It was the size of a watermelon. **How was it possible that I had not noticed it before?** It was hanging at eye-level and I had been there for hours!

It was beautiful — a papery, egg-shaped nest, with intricate layers of grays, browns, and whites. A flock of tiny songbirds was dancing about in the branches of the wasp-nest tree, issuing raspy, grating calls. They seemed upset and were all pointing their beaks at the nest.

All at once, the top section of the nest began to slowly rotate, much like the lid of a jar unscrewing itself. Then the top stopped turning and two eyes opened up — like big, black marbles — and stared right at me!

This was no wasps' nest — **it was a barred owl!** What had looked like a jar's lid was the owl's head. My jaw dropped in amazement.

The owl launched from its perch into the air, spread its softly feathered wings, and flew off. I watched its silent, buoyant flight through the understory until it disappeared in the verdant curtain of the forest's trees.

DEVIN (Green Frog)

SEEING LIKE AN OWL

Owls are masters of stillness and awareness. They perch on a branch and observe the world in utter stillness and silence. They can do this for so long that they seem to disappear to the world around them. As they sit, their wide-seeing eyes perceive tiny movements in the treetops or on the ground far below.

What would it be like to sit in such attentive stillness?

Stare at the dot on the next page while becoming aware of the other objects around you — a desk, a scene out the window, or the owl eye on this page. How many objects can you identify without taking your eyes off the dot?

Stare at the dot.

Looking in this way is called using your *peripheral vision.* As you focused on the dot, you at the same time expanded your awareness beyond it. When you add your imagination and envision yourself as an owl, you have put on your Owl Eyes.

Try using your peripheral vision once more, while becoming an owl in your imagination, right where you are, just as you did in Mind's Eye Imagining.

Picture a tree you would like to land in, and fly to it in your Mind's Eye.

Feel your feather-draped talons clamping securely around one of the tree's strong branches.

Notice the color of the sky (is it daytime or night?), and whether the tree is swaying in the wind.

Take in the interplay of sounds and silence.

From your perch in your Mind's Eye, imagine a distant object as your focal point, and practice using Owl Eyes.

GLIMPSE BIRDS

Today's activity will begin with practicing Owl Eyes at your Sit Spot. Then you will walk through your backyard using Owl Eyes to try to locate at least one bird. Your goal: to get close enough to the bird to see some of its colors or other markings.

BEFORE YOU BEGIN

As you begin this activity, be aware that some geographical locations, at certain times of the year or day, or in certain types of weather, truly have no bird activity.

Owl Eyes is a potent awareness tool. If you happen to return from today's activity having noticed no birds, you may be surprised to realize all the other things you *did* notice.

WHAT TO DO

1. **Go to your Sit Spot** and get comfortable. Pretend you are a fluffy owl, settling onto your perch. Use your Owl Eyes to gaze into your backyard, and see what you notice.

2. **Watch in your peripheral vision** for any bird movements. See if you can locate at least one backyard bird.

3. **If you locate a bird, Fox Walk** toward it. See if you can get close enough to observe its appearance and behavior. Give yourself at least twenty minutes for this step.

GAME OF THE DAY

SNAPSHOT

Before digital cameras, people took pictures and couldn't see them for a long time, until the film was developed. In this game your mind will be like a film camera. Using your Owl Eyes, take a mental "snapshot" of your surroundings. Keep your image safe inside your head until you return to this book. Then record the image by drawing a rough picture of what you saw in your journal.

REFLECTIONS

Think back on all the observations you made today using Owl Eyes. How did your body and mind feel while using this new way of seeing? Write about it in your journal.

O W L  IN THE CITY

Owl Eyes aren't just for "natural" landscapes. One evening while waiting for a city bus downtown, I gazed across the street at the bustling intersection using my Owl Eyes. Out of the corner of my eye, I saw a large shape swoop down out of a nearby tree. **I saw its striped belly as it flew over the heads of pedestrians, silently descended into a small park across the street, and quietly disappeared in the night.**

As traffic continued to stream by and people's feet continued to pound the pavement, I thought of how the rhythms of nature continue all around us, even when we are not paying attention. No one else seemed to notice the great horned owl in our midst that evening, and perhaps that is just the way the owl wanted it.
VALENTINA LUCCARDI (Firefly)

WHISTLES AND Giggles

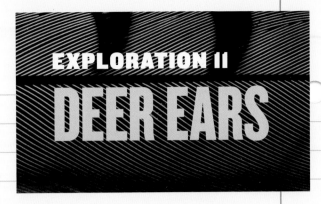

One February morning, I went outside to wander the backyard with my two-year-old son, Cedar. Mother Nature's icy nighttime slumber had turned into a deliciously warm day, an earth-scented breeze drifting above the snow-covered fields. I carried Cedar on my shoulders up a hill to a favorite white pine.

The dawn air danced with birdsong, and I showed him how to make Deer Ears. I cupped my hands behind my ears and then turned my head toward a birdcall to hear it better.

He watched and then imitated me, listening to the sounds around us. Every time we heard a new kind of birdcall, we appointed it a silly name to describe its unique sound.

We first heard a bold, clear whistle, sizzling the air like a laser gun: **DEEooo, DEEooo, DEEooo, Dew-Dew-Dew-Dew-Dew!** We decided to call this bird **laser bird.**

Next we heard a cheery canter that bounced through the air, as if saying: **a-PREA-cher! a-PREA-cher! a-PREA-cher! a-PREA-cher!** This one we nicknamed **preacher bird.**

Then we heard a soft, sweet birdcall, with a three-note voice calling out: **Cheese-bur-ger.** We named this bird **cheeseburger bird.**

With each new name we giggled harder and harder. These made-up nicknames taught us to pay closer attention to our backyard birds — and made us laugh all the way home.

DEVIN (Green Frog)

PUT ON YOUR
DEER EARS

Deer Ears can help you hear sounds in the woods much more clearly than your ordinary ears can. Here's how to make them.

WHAT TO DO

1. ***Make a circle with your two hands.*** Touch fingertips to fingertips and the heel of one palm to the heel of the other palm, leaving a round space in the middle.

2. ***Keeping that shape, place one hand completely behind each ear.*** This will sharpen your hearing.

3. ***Gently push your ears forward so they flare out.*** Make a tight seal with your hands. This will increase your hearing ability even more. Imagine you are a deer. *You've got your Deer Ears on!*

4. ***Using your Deer Ears, turn toward a sound*** and see what happens. Take your hands away, and see what happens then. Play with this a little to get used to it!

DESCRIBE A
BIRD SOUND

Today you'll use Deer Ears to listen to the wind, the rain, voices, traffic, and anything else that makes sound in your backyard. When you hear a birdcall, put on your Deer Ears to study the sound closely. Then come up with your own way to describe the sounds that bird is making.

WHAT TO DO

1. *Visit your Sit Spot and tune in* to the sounds of your backyard. Use Deer Ears to focus on any sounds that interest you (for example: *a horn beeping, frogs croaking,* or *the wind blowing*).

2. *When you hear a birdcall, use Deer Ears to home in on it.* If you do not hear a birdcall, use Deer Ears to make a slow sweep of your entire backyard from your Sit Spot. (If you still do not hear a birdcall, Wander around a bit in search of one.)

3. *Jot down some words* that *describe* the birdcall (for example: *soft, raucous, sweet, shrill, raspy, fast, rising, repetitive,* and so on) in your journal. If you hear no birdcalls, do this with any sound you do hear.

4. *Imitate the birdcall with your voice.* Write down words that sound like the call (for example: *meep-meep-meep; KEEeer! KEEeer!; BrrrrrrrOOP!;* and so on). Again, if you hear no birdcalls, do this with any sound.

KNOW
LOCAL BIRDS

Use the range maps in your field guide to find a bird that lives near you. As you learned in Exploration 7, a range map shows where a particular species lives.

Many birds live in more than one place during the year, though, and they travel back and forth, or *migrate*, in spring or fall. Those birds' range maps will have two or more colors on them — one for their winter (southern) range and one for their summer (northern) range. If your guide's maps show more than two colors, turn to the front of the book and learn what they represent.

WHAT YOU NEED

- Your field guide

WHAT TO DO

1. *Pick a bird, any bird,* in your bird field guide.

2. *Examine its range map,* and pinpoint where on the map you live.

3. *Notice what time of year* the bird is in the areas shown. Do any of the bird's ranges overlap with your location? If not, choose a different bird that does live in your area.

4. *Jot down your bird's name*, and make a quick, simple sketch of it.

SOUND OF SILLINESS

At some point today, listen to a sound being made somewhere in your surroundings. Listen as you normally would, and then try it with Deer Ears.

Study the sound in the same way you listened to the birdcall earlier today, asking yourself the same questions: *"How can I describe this sound using words? How can I write letters or words to imitate the sound?"* The words might seem silly, like *a-PREA-cher! a-PREA-cher! a-PREAcher! a-PREA-cher!* But be sure to give it a try.

How did listening to your surroundings change your awareness today? What did you discover as a result of using Deer Ears? Write about it in your journal.

SNEAKING UP ON FOXES

"It's the first week of May," I told my students. "Anybody want to watch a fox family raise its kits?" **Eyes wide with excitement, the response was unanimous: "Yeah!"**

"Okay," I said, "but we can't frighten the birds, otherwise they'll warn the foxes of our approach and we'll never see them. We will also need to approach the den from an unexpected direction. Oh — and one more thing — we'll have to cover ourselves in mud."

Eyes grew wider still. Mouths dropped open. **Five minutes later we all looked like swamp monsters in an old-time horror movie.** Smeared from head to toe in sticky black mud, we silently Fox Walked through the dappled gold-green cloak of a still-unfolding forest. Whenever we saw a bird, we stopped and patiently waited for it to leave of its own accord.

We emerged from the safe shadows of the forest, belly-crawled past my Sit Spot tree, and squeezed into the tiny shadow of a tiny, solitary willow tree. We could now see the fox den — an inconspicuous black hole in the face of a small forested hillside, across a narrow country dirt road from us. Lying in the mud like rotting, forgotten logs, we gazed at the den's entrance a stone's throw away.

Then something stirred on the hillside slope. Bursting out of the leaves, two fluffy orange fox kits pounced on each other and began to wrestle. A third and fourth emerged and joined the fun. A minute later, an adult fox trotted down the hill and disappeared into the black mouth of the den. **Camouflaged and silent, we were witnessing the life of a red fox family.**

Suddenly all four kits froze. Stock still, they stared for an instant down the dirt road. Then they scattered and simply melted into the earth, their own camouflaged coats blending perfectly with the leafy orange-brown earth. We exchanged glances, wondering what had frightened these cute kits into hiding. Did they notice something that we hadn't?

Two minutes later, we saw two pedestrians strolling down the road, chatting noisily. **They passed right between the fox den and our hiding spot, completely unaware that thirty feet into the forest lay a bunch of hiding kits, and thirty feet in the other direction lay a bunch of hiding kids!**

It took a full twenty minutes after the pedestrians had disappeared down the road for the fox kits to reappear and resume their play. We watched them a while longer, then quietly slipped away, retracing the route of our arrival. We Fox Walked back to base camp, washed the mud off our clothes and bodies in a stream, and gave each other high fives to celebrate our adventure in fox watching. This was a day we would never forget.

DEVIN (Green Frog)

LEARNING BIRD LANGUAGE

If you want to see more wildlife, you must pay attention to **Bird Language**. Bird Language is like a web of gossip that extends throughout the natural world. Most modern-living human beings travel through natural landscapes completely unaware of what birds are saying about them. They probably never learned the difference between *baseline* and *alarm*.

Baseline and Alarm

When teaching Bird Language, Tom Brown Jr. and Jon Young have us think of the natural landscape as a pond. When the landscape is peaceful, the pond is calm. This state is called *baseline*. When the landscape is disturbed, it is like a stone has dropped into the calm water and created a splash, with ripples that follow. This state is called *alarm*.

When danger shows up on a landscape, wildlife react by *alarming*. For example, when a hungry Cooper's hawk dashes into the forest in search of a meal, songbirds at the forest edge react with loud, bold alarm cries. This initial reaction is the splash.

Then wildlife deeper in the forest hear these alarm calls and issue their own. This is the ripple spreading from the splash. The ripple of alarm can continue deep into the forest.

The alarm won't continue forever, but it can travel far and fast enough to give wildlife time to hide — sometimes a full two minutes' worth. That is how the fox kits in the story could hide so early. After the pedestrians caused a splash by entering the forest, the ensuing bird alarm ripple may have escaped our awareness, but not that of the foxes! And alarm ripples can take up to twenty minutes to die down and allow baseline to return in the forest. This is why it took the foxes that long to reemerge.

If you want to see more wildlife, pay more attention to birds and "how they are doing." At any given moment, a bird — or any animal — is expressing either baseline or alarm. There are a number of ways we can determine whether a bird is in baseline or is alarming. The first way is to notice the bird's *voice*.

Voice

Have you ever listened to someone speak a language that you do not understand? Without understanding the words they are saying, you can guess how they feel. The sound of a person's — or a bird's — voice can say a lot about their possible mood or intentions.

The voice of an alarming bird can be any of the following:
- High-pitched
- Fast and insistent
- Loud
- Scratchy, screechy, harsh, or grating

HOW ALARM RIPPLES SPREAD

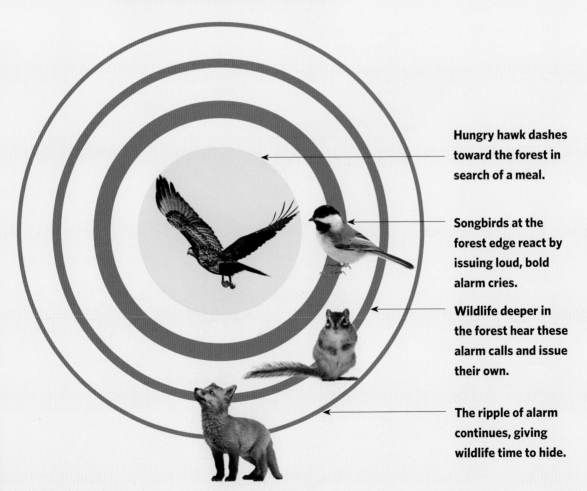

Hungry hawk dashes toward the forest in search of a meal.

Songbirds at the forest edge react by issuing loud, bold alarm cries.

Wildlife deeper in the forest hear these alarm calls and issue their own.

The ripple of alarm continues, giving wildlife time to hide.

Body Language

Have you ever watched a movie without sound? You can gather a lot of information about the characters without hearing their voices. Facial expressions and body language convey whether they are happy, sad, angry, afraid, and so on.

Similarly, an alarming bird might display one or more of the following types of body language:

- Tense, rigid posture
- Nervous flitting of wings and tail
- Craned neck, intently looking in a particular direction
- Cowering or hiding

With practice, you can use Bird Language to detect and locate the presence of a fox, a hawk, or even a human being in the forest *without ever seeing it*. The journey begins with the question, "How are my backyard birds doing?"

NOTICE
HAPPY BIRDS

Today your goal is simply to notice how your backyard birds are doing. Because birds aren't nature's only gossipers (Exploration 7 told of Stinker, the Sit Spot squirrel), pay attention to *all* your backyard wildlife — squirrels, neighborhood pets, humans, and even insects.

WHAT TO DO

1. *Fox Walk to your Sit Spot, settle in, and relax.* Spend a full twenty minutes there, not focusing on anything in particular. Just relax and enjoy what's around you.

2. *Listen to the voices* and observe the body language of any birds or other wildlife you see. Notice whether they seem disturbed or peaceful.

3. *Wander your backyard with no particular agenda* other than to notice your backyard birds and other wildlife and to consider, "How does it feel right now?"

GAME OF THE DAY

SILENT MOVIE

At some point today when you are near someone who is talking to someone else, cover your ears so you can no longer hear what he or she is saying. Pretend you are watching a silent movie.

As you watch, ask these simple questions: "What state is this person in, baseline or alarm? How can I tell?"

REFLECTIONS

What did you learn today about the world of birds in general, and about the birds around you? Write your thoughts in your journal.

Black BEAR

It was a warm August evening and we had opened all the doors and windows in my family's house to let the cool air in. I was in the kitchen, listening to the evening's birdsong symphony through the screened-in windows.

Suddenly the symphony turned into a cacophony of agitated bird alarms. Dinner would not be ready for a few minutes, so I stepped outside to see what was going on. The sun was setting, and it was almost dark out.

At first I did not see or hear anything unusual. Then, suddenly, the birds started alarming in a new location. I followed the sound until I heard a loud scraping noise coming from a tree in my neighbor's yard.

I turned toward the tree and saw a huge black bear sliding down its trunk! The bear hugged the bottom of the tree for a moment, rubbed itself against the bark, and then — completely ignoring me — got up and lumbered off.

Some of my best bird language experiences have happened simply because I decided to follow my curiosity out the door, and let the birds tell me where to look.

NICK SELTZER (Bat)

Two Ways of Walking

One sunny day in spring, I was walking along a forest trail with a million things on my mind. Despite my busy day ahead, I strolled at a relaxed pace, soaking in the freshness of the bright morning.

Soon I noticed an American robin perched on a lower branch of a tree near the trail. Not wanting to startle the bird, I took a deep breath, slowed my pace, and began to Fox Walk. **As I drew very close, the robin glanced at me, silently flew just a few feet off the trail, perched on a twig, and watched me pass.**

Then a group of three students approached from the opposite direction. They walked quickly, with their heads facing downward, talking loudly, and playing music from a smartphone. As they passed me, I turned to see how the robin might respond to their presence. As they unknowingly drew closer, it launched from its perch and flew off, alarming.

— *Leo Proechel (Ladybug)*

yeep

YOUR BACKYARD BIRDS

How has Expanding the Senses by using **Owl Eyes** and **Deer Ears** and listening for **Bird Language** affected your interactions with your backyard birds? Write your thoughts in your journal.

This chapter offered new skills to help you tune in to the fascinating world of birds and interact with this world in new ways.

Your Backyard Community

The members of our backyard community are all connected to one another — and to us. Chapter 5 will give you a broader view of your backyard, and of the neighbors you have discovered there throughout this journey.

IN EXPLORATION 13, you will use **Journaling** to identify the connections that bind your backyard neighbors together.

IN EXPLORATION 14, you will strengthen your connections with your human community by sharing a personal **Story of the Day** with a person of your choice.

IN EXPLORATION 15, you will deepen your connection with your backyard by **Giving Thanks,** reflecting on the backyard knowledge, experiences, and wisdom you have gained while taking this journey.

Let's get started!

Manzanita Café

Michelle and I began our friendship at college in Arizona, where we practiced Sit Spot, Wandering, Tracking, and Bird Language in the scrubby local desert. One day we explored my backyard: an arid hillside of juniper, pine, and oak scrub, dotted with ancient boulders the size of cars. We loved the idea that "everything in nature is connected," but we wanted to discover this with our very own senses, by observing true connections between the real and wild beings we called our neighbors. We wanted to see the web for ourselves.

We left my back lawn and followed a narrow, winding animal trail into the chaparral. Our boots crunched past worn granite boulders and dusty ceanothus bushes. We stopped. **Out of the desert silence came the barely audible sound of small seeds being cracked open by a hard beak.** The sound was coming from the dense shade of a nearby shrub we recognized as a manzanita. Was it a bird, hiding in the manzanita bush and foraging on its tiny seeds? We decided to investigate.

Fox Walking slowly toward the bush, we got quite close when

a raspy voice rang out from within its tangled shadows: *Shhwreeep?!* A bird with a black head and wings, a white belly, and orange on its sides peeked out from the manzanita bush into

the harsh sunlight. It glanced at us with deep red eyes, then flew off, pumping its wings and tail until it was out of sight. It was a spotted towhee — a seed-eating bird common to this Arizona desert — now disturbed by our curiosity. Could this have been the source of the seed-cracking sounds we had heard?

Michelle and I got down on our hands and knees to investigate the tangle of smooth, burgundy-colored branches and olive-green leaves. Sure enough, strewn beneath its spreading branches were bits of manzanita seeds, freshly nibbled. This was our first tangible link between two of our backyard neighbors — a towhee enjoying the shelter and food offered by a manzanita bush! **We could imagine a rope of connection binding towhee and manzanita together.**

We backed out of the manzanita maze and returned to the animal trail. A few steps up the path we encountered a boulder the size of a washing machine, severed completely in two by time and weather. Peering into a deep crack, we saw on the dim ground another pile of chewed manzanita seeds. But these were clearly torn open by tiny teeth, not crushed open by a hard beak. Who was this mysterious second fan of the manzanita seeds?

Squinting hard, we made out the rice-shaped, black scats of a mouse, mixed in with the pale seeds. So towhee and mouse were both customers of the manzanita café! The rope of connection

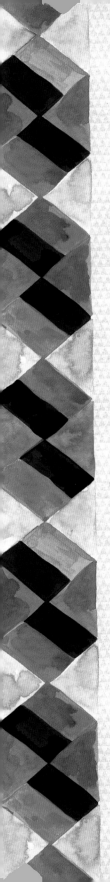

extended now among three neighbors — towhee, manzanita, and mouse.

Michelle and I wondered: *What would it be like if we were this tiny mouse dining in the shelter of this cloven rock, a mere few inches from such a well-used animal trail?* We could picture a passing fox or coyote snapping up the hapless mouse in its jaws for a snack. Curious now, we scanned the trail, looking for clues left behind by either one of these rodent-eating wild canids.

Seconds later, we found one: a fresh twist of coyote scat lying casually on the trailside. **We easily imagined a hungry coyote pawing into the cracked rock for our trapped little mouse.** We didn't need to pry mouse bones from a coyote scat to confirm this age-old relationship — but we did anyway. What poured out was not mouse bones, but the half-digested, blueberry-like fruits from an alligator juniper tree.

We checked our watches. It was time to head to class. The links we had just traced among our backyard neighbors were so tangible, yet completely unseen. We could almost see them, however — silver strands of a spider's web shimmering in the empty air, extending from towhee to manzanita to mouse to coyote to juniper . . . and beyond.

We gazed at the scene we were about to leave. The lumpy, scraggly landscape seemed to glow with a new light, illuminating a single word: community.

— *Devin (Green Frog)*

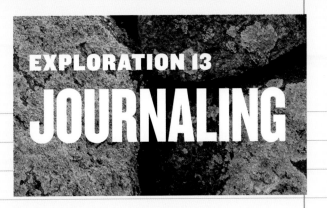

For the last few days I have been thinking about going out in the morning to try to feed the chickadees by hand. My dad and I have been trying to feed them by hand for so long. This morning I woke up at 7:23 a.m., got dressed, and went out to the deck with a handful of sunflower seeds. I sat in a chair and stretched out my arm on the armrest. As I opened my hand one of the seeds stuck to my finger and lay just beyond my hand. Ten seconds later, a chickadee flew down to a nearby railing. I did not move. I just watched.

The chickadee flew down toward my hand but when it was only inches away and I had my hopes up, it turned and flew back to the railing. It repeated this a few times. Then it happened! The chickadee flew down, landed on the end of the armrest, took the seed from my finger, and quickly flew off to the safety of the bushes with the seed in its beak. I was so happy!

A few minutes later it was back. **It hopped onto my hand,** took a seed, looked around a bit, swallowed it, looked around again, picked up another seed, and flew off. This time, I was so, so happy!

When it returned just a minute or two later, I noticed its right foot was badly injured. Most chickadees' feet have three toes with little talons in the front and one toe with a slightly bigger talon in the back.

But this chickadee's right foot's first toe bent back against the bottom of its foot, and its middle and third toes were shorter stubs. Its left foot looked as I would expect.

When this chickadee was on the deck, it would not let any other birds share the space. There was another chickadee that came a few times. I noticed that both of its feet looked as I would expect. This chickadee was a little braver each time it came by.

At about 8:00 a.m. I went inside because my fingers were cold. I told Mom, Dad, and my brother Will about the birds, and they all said they wanted to see them. So we all went outside and they saw what I had seen, except that they could not see the first bird's injured foot very well.

These are the living creatures I saw other than Mom, Dad, Will, and the chickadees: a squirrel in the yard, crows, a nuthatch, many sparrows, a hawk, tufted titmice, bluebirds, and two downy woodpeckers.

TOMMY KIRBY (Chipmunk)

REVEALING ROOTS

The Core Routine of **Journaling** means telling stories by documenting and reflecting on your experiences, an excellent way to deepen your roots in nature.

You probably guessed that you've already been Journaling — every day throughout this entire book! You've jotted down answers to questions, dreamed up new questions, sketched wildlife in the field and from memory, recorded information from a field guide, noted personal nature experiences, and reflected on these experiences in writing. These are all examples of Journaling.

Until now, you have been given structure for your Journaling process, with questions and prompts to get you started and guide you. Now it is time to practice Journaling unbounded by rules — or, more accurately, bounded only by the rules you choose to apply.

SIT SPOT JOURNALING

Today is the first day of the final chapter of this book. Since Exploration 1, you have made twelve trips to your Sit Spot and practiced twelve different kinds of Core Routines. You have taken quite a journey of increasing knowledge, awareness, and connection!

Today you will revisit the same, timeless activity you completed in that very first Exploration: the simple practice of sitting in nature and observing your surroundings. Although the central activity will be the same, your experience of awareness and connection to your backyard has changed on a number of levels.

WHAT TO DO

1. *Sit at your Sit Spot and observe* your backyard for at least ten minutes. Settle in and use your senses to take in your surroundings. What do you notice?

2. *When you return home, write or sketch* your observations, thoughts, feelings, and questions, using prose, poetry, objective observations, drawing, mapping, or any other method to record your experience.

SIT SPOT SHOPPING

As we have traveled along on this journey, you have been learning how much a single Sit Spot area can increase your awareness of your entire backyard. Sometime today, as you pass by a natural space outdoors — such as a backyard, a park, or a vacant lot — ask yourself, "If that were my backyard, where would I want my Sit Spot to be?"

REFLECTIONS

Turn back to the notes you wrote after visiting your Sit Spot in Exploration 1, and read through them. How does it feel to look back on your first Exploration in this book? In what ways have you grown as an observer of your surroundings? How has Journaling as a daily Core Routine played a part in this growth? Write about it in your journal.

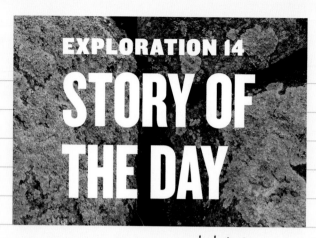

EXPLORATION 14
STORY OF THE DAY

PAYING ATTENTION

As a Flying Deer Nature Center staffer, I've learned how sharing stories about personal nature experiences can actually affect your relationship with nature. **In one camp, we practiced the "dynamic duo" of Core Routines: Sit Spot in the early morning and Story of the Day during breakfast.** During the sharing circle, campers shared what they saw out at their Sit Spots.

On Monday morning, the campers were all excited to get out to their Sit Spots. When they returned, their stories were energetic, enthusiastic, and very short: "When I was walking to my Sit Spot I saw a squirrel. It was awesome!" "At my Sit Spot I saw a bird. It was beautiful!" During each story's telling, the campers seemed more anxious to spout their own stories than to listen to the one being told.

By Wednesday morning, campers were even more excited. Two days of storytelling had whetted their appetite for Sit Spots even more — and they now paid more attention at their Sit Spots.

The stories in the sharing circle became more elaborate. The camper who on Monday saw a squirrel reported seeing another one today. Now he shared how it reacted when he walked toward it, what route it took up the tree, and so on. The camper who earlier saw a bird this time described seeing it, listening to its song, and wondering why it sang that particular song, at that particular moment.

In addition to paying more attention at their Sit Spots, the campers began paying more attention to each other's stories. Sharing circles became webs of discussion. Campers asked questions of the storyteller, responded to one another's stories, and discovered how their experiences interconnected.

By Friday morning, the staff sat back, amazed at the level of listening and storytelling that had developed during five days, five Sit Spots, and five Stories of the Day.

TOPAZ ROSS KELSO

(Lynx)

SHARING MOMENTS

Whenever you share a nature experience in the form of a story, something magical happens. The experience ripens like a delicious fruit, and inside it grows a seed for a future nature experience. This is what the Core Routine **Story of the Day** is all about.

When you Journal you tell a Story of the Day with paper and a writing or drawing instrument. Reading this book you told stories through Journaling every time you documented your backyard, sketched one of its inhabitants, or wrote about a backyard experience. You may have noticed that writing or drawing strengthened your connection to the beings and places in your backyard and everyday life.

Long ago (and still today), humans around the globe would gather at day's end — perhaps around a flickering fire — to share the stories of the day. Everyone was both a *storyteller*, with deep and curious listeners, and a *listener* to extraordinary tales. The web of community grew stronger and the members' desire for adventure and discovery grew.

The word *community* is also used by scientists to describe the web of relationships among plants, animals, soil, water, and weather in a natural place. One mark of health in the natural world is a diversity of wildlife species and a wealth of relationships among them.

In this activity you will identify two kinds of community — the *natural community* found in your backyard, and the *human community* found throughout your life. You will do this by creating two maps:

- **A Backyard Community Map** that reflects the web of relationships in your backyard
- **A Human Community Map** that highlights certain relationships within your human community

Together, these maps will show you both the threads that connect various beings in your backyard and the ones that connect you with the people in your life.

MAP YOUR BACKYARD COMMUNITY

The natural world within your backyard that you have been exploring throughout this book is filled with a myriad of characters. Many interact with one another regularly, some for a long time. Each character that you can see or sense from there — the trees, mammals, birds, soil, wind, and stars —is a member of your backyard community.

For today's activity, begin by visiting your Sit Spot and thinking of some of the members of your backyard community. Include not only living members (birds, mammals, trees, or other beings you have observed there), but also non-living members (streams, boulders, patches of bare earth, buildings, the wind, and so on).

WHAT TO DO

1. *From your Sit Spot,* use your senses to observe backyard community members can you notice with your senses? Make a map of them in your journal. Be sure to include your Sit Spot area, your New Neighbor tree, and yourself!

2. *From your Sit Spot, think back* over all of your backyard experiences in this book. Add any other backyard community members you encountered, living or non-living, to the map.

3. *Wander your backyard,* adding any more community members that you see or recall to your list.

4. *Think of a connection* between any two community members you have listed. Draw a line between their names, and write a short description of the connection on that line. Repeat for as many other connections as you would like.

MAP YOUR
HUMAN
COMMUNITY

Like a natural community, a human community can have many members — family, friends, teachers, neighbors, coaches, elders, and so on — with unique relationships connecting them all. In the next portion of today's activity, you will create a community map that identifies your favorite personal stories of the day, and highlights any individuals in your life who have played — or might be willing to play — the role of a village elder, by listening to one of those stories.

In my community, Lenny Brown, a founder of Flying Deer Nature Center, is an example of an elder. I love to visit him and tell him personal stories — especially about my adventures in nature. Part of why I love telling him stories is because he loves listening to them. He always asks me one or two good questions — and sometimes more — to draw the details out of me, and he responds to my tales with genuine excitement.

WHAT TO DO

1. *Think of a few people in your life* that you feel are good listeners: they enjoy hearing your stories, ask good questions, or make you feel at ease when you are sharing. Write the names of one or more people who come to mind and list them on the left side of a fresh page in your journal.

2. *Think about all of the stories* you have gathered about your backyard adventures while journeying through this book. Create a simple title for each one, and list them on the right side of the page.

3. *Make connections* between your listeners and your stories. *Which of the people you listed would enjoy hearing which of your backyard adventure stories?* Draw a line connecting the stories and the listeners.

GAME OF THE DAY

BACKYARD SHARED

Sometime today, ask someone if you can tell them a story about an experience you had while using this book. Your story can be as long or as short as you would like. *Have fun!*

REFLECTIONS

Having great adventures is a wonderful way to connect with nature, but it is only half of the nature connection process. Experience leads to reflection, and reflection leads to further experience. Looking back on this book, how have your reflections deepened your connection with your backyard?

STREAM OF Joy

I once lived in a house nestled inside the heart of a mountain, on the edge of a forest where I could play at any time.

A small stream spilled down the mountainside. Every day after school my friends and I ran to the stream to splash in the cool water and escape from the hot sun. **I remember those days fondly — splashing water into the air and screaming with delight, constructing dams with rocks and mud, and racing twigs down the rolling current.**

A distinct sense of happiness and joviality danced through the air, especially when someone fell into the water. When we dragged our dripping bodies up and out of the stream to bask in the last warming rays of the sun, I felt truly happy and truly alive.

A certain feeling was present at such times. It was a feeling of great joy, an awareness of something bubbling up inside my soul, which could only be released through laughter. It was a great passion for living, which made me long to jump to my feet and whirl about — a certain emotion that made everything I witnessed beautiful to behold. **It was an overwhelming thankfulness for all that was around me.**

That feeling, that emotion, I believe, was gratitude, for gratitude is not just saying a prayer before eating a meal. Gratitude, in its most pure form, is a great unity with all of the energy filling the space around us. In short, gratitude is love.

BEN ZOELLER (Chickadee)

CELEBRATING CONNECTION

The final Core Routine of this book is **Giving Thanks**. Cultures around the world understand and practice this. It's simple: get in touch with your gratitude and express it — and feel free to do it in your own unique way!

A Thanksgiving Address

For eons, before any important gathering, the First Nations people who call themselves the Haudenosaunee — also known as the People of the Longhouse or the Iroquois of present-day New York state — have given a Thanksgiving Address.

The Haudenosaunee freely share this gratitude practice with others to help us deepen our connections with the earth, each other, and ourselves. They ask that we adapt the practice to suit our own communities.

Tekaronieneken Jake Swamp (1940–2010), from the Akwesasne Mohawk community and the Tree of Peace Society, shared with us the importance of giving thanks. We at Flying Deer Nature Center have adopted and adapted it as our most formal way to offer our gratitude as we open special occasions and events. When we give a formal Thanksgiving Address, we often incorporate many of these approaches:

- We speak words of thankfulness, either silently or out loud, to the many different facets of the world around us.
- We may address any or all of these facets: the humans, the earth, the waters, the creatures that live in the waters, the soil and rocks, the green growing plants, the insects and other creeping crawlers, the animals, the trees, the birds, the winds, the four directions (east, south, west, and north), the rain and other weather, the sun, the moon, the stars, the Creative Power, our ancestors, the future generations, and an encompassing gratitude to everything we cherish that we did not mention.
- These facets are sometimes broad (for example, *to the people of all the world,* or *to all the trees*). Or we can express a deeper, more personal gratitude (for example, *to sister,* or *to my Sit Spot tree*).
- We address these facets of nature, humanity, and the elements as if they are here with us, listening to our heartfelt words.
- As we speak to each facet of the world around us, we have the chance to summon beautiful, moving images in our Mind's Eye. They in turn can help us get in touch with our deepest gratitude.

As you walk through today's activity, feel free to use the style we present here, create your own variation, or create your own way of Giving Thanks all together.

How you give thanks, how long you spend doing so, and where you go to express your gratitude are all up to you. Enjoy this process, as it can create a very special experience.

GIVE A
THANKSGIVING ADDRESS

In today's activity you will complete your backyard nature journey. Your intention is to create closure by getting in touch with your gratitude.

WHAT TO DO

1. *Visit your Sit Spot.* Settle in and relax.

2. *Let your gratitude surface.* Ask yourself, "Where in my body, heart, or mind do I feel gratitude right now?" Feel your thanks for what you have experienced during this journey, and for any help (nature, people, or the elements) that has been a part of your process.

3. *Wander your backyard,* continuing to experience your gratitude in any way that feels right to you.

4. *Take a few minutes* to express your gratitude in your journal.

GAME OF THE DAY

THANK YOU

At some point today, find someone or something to whom you are grateful, and say "thank you." Then say more about why you feel thankful for having this person or thing in your life.

REFLECTIONS

How did the Core Routine of **Giving Thanks** affect how you feel about your backyard, the natural world, yourself, and the other facets of your world? Write your thoughts in your journal.

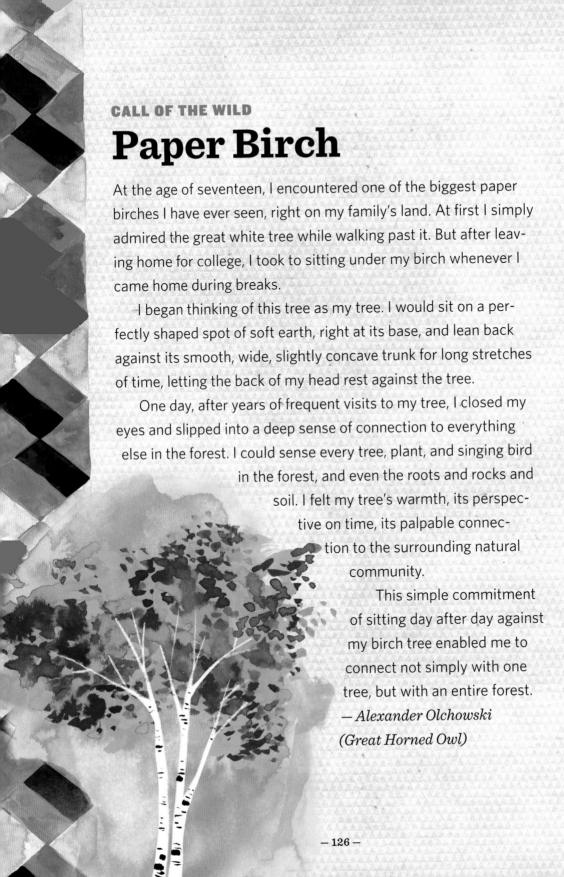

Paper Birch

At the age of seventeen, I encountered one of the biggest paper birches I have ever seen, right on my family's land. At first I simply admired the great white tree while walking past it. But after leaving home for college, I took to sitting under my birch whenever I came home during breaks.

I began thinking of this tree as my tree. I would sit on a perfectly shaped spot of soft earth, right at its base, and lean back against its smooth, wide, slightly concave trunk for long stretches of time, letting the back of my head rest against the tree.

One day, after years of frequent visits to my tree, I closed my eyes and slipped into a deep sense of connection to everything else in the forest. I could sense every tree, plant, and singing bird in the forest, and even the roots and rocks and soil. I felt my tree's warmth, its perspective on time, its palpable connection to the surrounding natural community.

This simple commitment of sitting day after day against my birch tree enabled me to connect not simply with one tree, but with an entire forest.

— *Alexander Olchowski*
(Great Horned Owl)

YOUR BACKYARD COMMUNITY

Chapter 5 helped you find connections among your various backyard neighbors, think of your backyard as a natural community, and deepen your connection with both your natural and human communities.

How have the Core Routines of **Journaling**, **Story of the Day**, and **Giving Thanks** helped you expand your understanding of your backyard and human communities, and how you feel part of them? Write your thoughts in your journal.

Your Backyard Journey Continues

Revisiting the Core Routines of Nature Connection

Working through this book is indeed a journey, and you have traveled a long way. In chapter 1, you opened your eyes to a new backyard; in chapter 2, you began to dismantle the Wall of Green; in chapter 3, you popped your awareness bubbles; in chapter 4, you drew back the curtains of your backyard stage; and in chapter 5, you traced the web of your backyard community's relationships. You have accomplished so much since beginning this journey!

Let's look back at how you accomplished these things.

- *You deepened your awareness* of your backyard by visiting your **Sit Spot** each day.

- *You explored your backyard* as if for the first time through **Wandering.**

- *You surveyed* your backyard habitats through **Mapping.**

- *You noticed the patterns* of shape, color, and texture in your backyard trees through **Engaging the Senses.**

- *You met a New Neighbor tree* through **Exploring a Field Guide.**

- *You pictured your backyard trees* from above through **Mind's Eye Imagining.**

- *You learned how to move quietly* by **Fox Walking.**

- *You pondered the secret lives* of your backyard mammals through **Questioning.**

- *You investigated clues* and mysteries left by your backyard mammals by **Tracking.**

- *You glimpsed elusive backyard birds* using **Owl Eyes.**

- *You tuned in to the unique sounds* of your backyard birds using **Deer Ears.**

- *You eavesdropped* on bird conversations by listening for **Bird Language.**

- *You traced connections* in your backyard's natural community through **Journaling.**

- *You shared your adventures* and discoveries with your human community through **Story of the Day.**

- *You offered gratitude* for your backyard journey by **Giving Thanks.**

You have truly covered a lot of ground! Using the Core Routines as your guide, you reached *a deeper understanding of yourself and the natural world* around you.

This book was designed to give you fifteen days' worth of Core Routine practices. If you particularly enjoyed certain Core Routines, continue to use them again and again! When you weave them into your life, *that's when the deeper magic begins to happen.* As you practice them over time, you may find moments when it feels less like you are practicing the Core Routines and more like the Core Routines are practicing you.

REFLECTING ON THE JOURNEY

The word *ecology* comes from a Greek term meaning "house" or "dwelling place." How have the Core Routines and this book as a whole helped you to create an inner place of awareness, connection, and appreciation for the natural world of which you are a part?

The Barred Owl

One winter afternoon, I realized that I had not practiced Sit Spot in some time and felt something was missing from my life. I set out from my house into my New England backyard with a plan to Wander the landscape until I found a good Sit Spot. I took a trail into the thick forest and Wandered into an enormous field.

Across the field stood a dense wall of young white pine trees, impenetrable except for one small break — **an enchanting archway, a tunnel into the forest. I entered the tunnel.**

As I emerged from the tunnel's other side, I encountered fresh deer prints and began Tracking them through the forest. The trail led to a small stream and turned. I followed them upstream. Around a large bend, I discovered a towering cliff three stories high, topped with trees, with the stream rushing along its base.

Standing inside the stream's bend, I felt an overwhelming surge of happiness and gratitude. I heard in my mind: *This is the best place ever!* I looked around more deeply. An owl was perched nearby! It was a very large barred owl, sitting on a fallen tree just a few feet off the ground, about twenty feet from me. I sat down and watched it for what seemed like an eternity.

I could tell the owl was relaxed despite my presence. It simply looked in my direction every once in a while and blinked. At one point it even closed its eyes and appeared to take a little nap! Interestingly, the Bird Language in the surrounding forest was calm and peaceful.

I decided to Fox Walk toward the owl, to get a closer look. Ever so slowly I moved closer, each step taking two minutes to complete. After about twenty minutes I was less than ten feet from the owl. I sat down and studied the intricate details of its feathers, the color of its eyes, and the movement of its chest as it breathed in and out. In that moment I was filled with an energy and vitality that I can only describe as *owl-ness*.

Eventually I heard a clang of metal striking metal, perhaps from someone's yard. The owl turned its head toward the sound, crouched, and sprang into the air, flying silently off into the forest.

I was filled with gratitude and an abundance of energy in my body. I felt fully alive and deeply connected to the mystery of life as though some essential part of myself had been restored.

I later shared this story with Devin. He pointed out that my backyard adventure included not just Sit Spot, but a number of other Core Routines of Nature Connection as well. While I was focused on one Core Routine as my goal, the others slipped in and aided me in reconnecting with nature.

When I first heard of the Core Routines, they seemed foreign — even disruptive — to my normal ways of being. But soon, especially when I practiced several of them together, they became second nature. They slowly increased my capacity for awareness of my surroundings, and before long they simply became a part of me, feeding a natural way of living life: with awareness, connection, gratitude, wonder, and awe toward the world.

— *Nur Habib Tiven (Grouse)*

THE BACKYARD QUIZ

Before and after you take this journey, use your journal to answer these questions about your backyard. This is a way of recognizing and celebrating the knowledge you will gain and have gained while working your way through this book.

Feel free to write "I don't know," if you do not know the answer to a question. Recognizing what we do not know is a great strength, because it can open doors to further learning. As always, you are right where you need to be in this journey.

---

1. Name a kind of tree that grows in your backyard, and draw a picture of this tree's leaf.

2. What kinds of foxes, if any, live in your part of the country?

3. If a fox were to visit your backyard, where do you think it would like to hide?

4. Name a kind of bird that lives in or passes through your area.

5. At what time(s) of year can this bird be found in your area?

6. Draw a simple picture of this bird. Write two things one could notice about this bird, to help identify it.

7. What kinds of habitats can be found in your backyard?

8. Draw a simple sketch of your backyard, as if you were looking down from above.

9. Write the name of a creature that lives in or passes through your backyard. Then write one type of recognizable clue it leaves behind on the landscape (some sign that tells you it was there), and make a sketch of this clue.

10. Write the names of two things in your backyard that are connected to each other through some type of relationship or interaction, then briefly describe this relationship or interaction.

OWL EYES CERTIFICATION

As a way of recognizing the great accomplishment of completing the reading, exercises, and activities offered in this book, Flying Deer Nature Center offers Certificates of Course Completion. Receiving a certificate is a great way to honor your dedication to completing this journey, symbolize your knowledge and understanding of your backyard's natural community, and remember that you are an integral part of that community.

To submit your work for review, please photocopy the pages you have filled out in your journal:

- Worksheets and Reflections (Explorations 1 to 15)
- Chapter Reflections (chapters 1 to 5)

- Extra pages you used for notes or Journaling or Game of the Day
- A written request for a Certificate of Course Completion

Materials can then be mailed with a processing fee of fifteen dollars to:

> *Put On Your Owl Eyes*
>> *Certificate Requests*
> **Flying Deer Nature Center**
> *122 Daley Road*
> *East Chatham, NY 12060*

If you prefer to scan and submit your pages electronically, please send them to: info@flyingdeernaturecenter.org

We look forward to receiving coursework from students all across North America and beyond.

SPEAKING METRIC

1 inch = 2.54 centimeters
1 foot = 30.5 centimeters
1 yard = 0.9 meter
1 mile = 1.6 kilometers

CONNECTIONS

If you want to learn more about nature connection, here are some organizations and resources that can guide you.

Flying Deer Nature Center is an outdoor education organization nestled in rural Columbia County near East Chatham, New York. Our mission is to educate and mentor children and adults in deep connection to nature, self, and community by engaging participants in naturalist routines, survival skills, wilderness rites of passage, and community-building activities.
www.flyingdeernaturecenter.org

The 8 Shields Institute, founded by expert naturalist and tracker Jon Young, has developed training pathways over decades that support mentors and leaders in traditional mentoring and deep nature connection practices.
www.8shields.org

Bird Language Leaders is an endeavor designed to awaken deep nature connection in people of all ages through understanding the bird communication patterns in a landscape. It is being offered in 60 locations nationwide and in other parts of the world, in collaboration with nature centers, schools, and universities.
www.birdlanguage.com

The Kamana Naturalist Training Program was created by Jon Young to model the process by which he was mentored by renowned naturalist Tom Brown, Jr. as a boy. In this experiential four-level home study course students become confident naturalists, melding modern field ecology with the skills of a native scout.
www.wildernessawareness.org/kamana

The Art of Mentoring is a weeklong experiential nature-based program, available worldwide, teaching participants to remember the ways of our ancestors and apply them to our modern communities. The intention is that we once again live in healthy, regenerative communities — villages where people of all ages are in deep relationship with the land, each other, and themselves.
www.8shields.org/art-of-mentoring

Coyote's Guide to Connecting with Nature, by Jon Young, passes on the subtle nature-based educational methods that were used long ago, when subsistence lifestyles kept humankind close to the natural cycles of the earth. It presents the Core Routines of Nature Connection, as well as a comprehensive collection of educational tools to foster connection to nature, community, and self.
www.coyotesguide.com

What the Robin Knows: How Birds Reveal the Secrets of the Natural World, by Jon Young, unites indigenous knowledge, up-to-date research, and Young's nature experiences spanning four decades to lead us toward a deeper connection with animals and with ourselves.
www.whattherobinknows.com

The Tracker is the epic autobiographical story of Tom Brown Jr.'s initial encounter and subsequent decade of apprenticeship with Grandfather, an Apache scout and tracker of astonishing physical and spiritual capabilities. This book's lessons have become a model for discovery, learning, and transformation in nature for hundreds of nature schools across the globe.
www.penguinrandomhouse.com

The Tracker School, founded in 1978 by Tom Brown Jr., offers powerful courses in tracking, scout, traditional healing, vision, and wilderness survival skills, both on location and online, that change the lives of students of all ages.

www.trackerschool.com

Organizations Affiliated with Flying Deer Nature Center

The Abode of the Message
New Lebanon, NY
www.theabode.org

Earthwalk Vermont
Plainfield, VT
www.earthwalkvermont.org

Earthwork Programs
Williamsburg, MA
www.earthworkprograms.com

Institute for Natural Learning
Brattleboro, VT
www.ifnaturallearning.com

Living Earth School
Afton, VA
www.livingearthva.com

Mountain Road School
New Lebanon, NY
www.mountainroadschool.org

Primitive Pursuits
Ithaca, NY
www.primitivepursuits.com

Sassafras
Aquinnah, MA
www.sassafrasmvy.org

Tamakoce Wilderness School
Petersburgh, NY
www.tamakocewildernessprograms.com

Tracker School
Watertown, NJ
www.trackerschool.com

Two Coyotes
Monroe, CT
www.twocoyotes.org

Vermont Wilderness School
Brattleboro, VT
www.vermontwildernessschool.org

White Pine Programs
York, ME
www.whitepineprograms.org

Wild Earth
High Falls, NY
www.wildearth.org

Wilderness Awareness School
Duvall, WA
www.wildernessawareness.org

Woodland Ways
Philmont, NY
www.woodlandways.com

INDEX

Page numbers in *italic* indicate drawings/illustrations and photographs.